LEARNING TO TEACH PRACTICAL SKILLS

A Self-instruction Guide

Second Edition

Ian Winfield

Kogan Page Ltd, London
Nichols Publishing Company,
New York

First edition published in Great Britain by
Kogan Page Limited and distributed
in the United States of America by
Nichols Publishing Company in 1979

This second edition first published in
Great Britain in 1988 by Kogan Page Limited,
120 Pentonville Road, London N1 9JN

British Library Cataloguing in Publication Data

Winfield, Ian
    Learning to teach practical skills. —
    2nd ed.
    1. Ability — Study and teaching
    I. Title
    153.9   BF431

    ISBN 1-85091-447-8

This second edition first published in
the United States of America in 1988 by
Nichols Publishing Company, PO Box 96,
New York, NY 10024

Library of Congress Cataloging-in-Publication Data

Winfield, Ian.
    Learning to teach practical skills/Ian Winfield. – – 2nd ed.
        p.   cm.
    Bibliography: p.
    ISBN 0-89397-292-4 : $20.00 (est.)
    1. Life skills – – Study and teaching.   I. Title.
  HQ2037.W56 1988
  362.6'3 – – dc19   87-22320
                                                         CIP

Printed and bound in Great Britain by Biddles Ltd,
Guildford, Surrey

Contents

Introduction to the second edition

Suddenly the fact that there is a chronic skills shortage has been realized. Practical skills are part of the wide range of basic skills needed in production, manufacturing, maintenance and repair. They demand time, forethought, craft and a degree of human pride. This book is about how we teach these practical skills to one another.

In my opinion this class of practical skills has been over-looked by government and industry alike. It is easy to see why. For several years the focus has been on high technology skills, on structural changes in employment and the emergence of the so-called service industries. In this respect, the simple fact that most of the wealth-creation in current industry still depends upon relatively humble practical skills, has been overlooked. The result of such a shortage should be obvious: there are not enough people with the ability and know-how to maintain present standards of living. We should ask how this is so.

For the individual this skilled labour shortage manifests itself when we search for someone to repair or renovate our property — be it our home, car or domestic appliance. The booming 'Do-It-Yourself' industry has grown up on the back of this state of affairs. At the company level bald statistics provide the necessary information: one in five companies report a shortage of skilled workers. Nationally, there is the dawning awareness of new challenges from overseas, many countries are learning new, production-related skills faster and more effectively than we in the UK are. An in-depth exam-ination of this sad state of affairs is beyond the scope of this book. Here I am concerned with both the methods by which we instruct practical skills and the setting or context in which this instruction is undertaken.

The first edition of this book was unashamedly driven by

ideas which were themselves the product of 1960s thinking, nurtured by the experience of the 1970s. The philosophy was that we had no need for professional teachers, instructors or tutors for we could teach ourselves to teach. Teachers could swap skills in free exchange. Skill exchange networks, it was argued, could then extend beyond the confines of the college, training centre, or workshop. State-accredited instructors, teaching diplomas and credentials would be superfluous under this scheme. The message was youthfully optimistic — all you needed was a little co-operation and a Kogan Page Self Instruction Guide.

From the perspective of the late 1980s such idealism seems quaint or downright romantic, for today radical changes in the contexts in which people learn new skills are taking place. There is not less, but more state intervention to which the burgeoning amount of state-run schemes bear witness. However, the current economic climate seems to have brought about a curious time-loop, bringing us right back to the original goal of the First Edition. Instructor training is now almost prohibitively costly and tight company budgetary control limits expensive training in instructional techniques for trainers and managers. The teach yourself technique has once more found favour but this time for different reasons.

Society has not stood still either; the social and political context in which skill instruction takes place today presents new challenges and opportunities. It is these new challenges and opportunities which I have endeavoured to cover in this Second Edition. Above all, there is today a new openess in the market for learning new skills. Restrictive practices on entry to trades and jobs has been reduced, and unemployment or the fear of it makes people just a little more eager to learn. Traditional barriers of sex, age and ethnic divides are being crossed in an open and welcome manner. I have therefore concentrated on explaining how to make contact with people and how to overcome communication barriers.

Today's instructor requires not only sound analytic ability but also developed social skills in crossing barriers, in overcoming learner underachievement, and in making genuine human contact.

NB: Where the male pronoun has been used it is for stylistic reasons only and covers both masculine and feminine genders.

Chapter 1
Sharing our skills

Overview: This first chapter looks at the origins of our attitudes to instruction, how these attitudes show themselves and how we might begin to change them. It goes on to look at where and how most practical instruction takes place. There have been some important changes in this field in the past few years. These changes are discussed and the scope of the rest of the book is briefly outlined.

Why are our skills important?

The most valuable possessions that each one of us will ever own are ours already: these are our own individual skills, talents and abilities. What we can already do now is what really counts. Not what we would like to be able to do or learn sometime in the future, but right here, *now*.

These are our true assets, our most valued possessions worth more than any amount of wealth or property. Just suppose that we lost all our personal property, we lost our jobs, our incomes. Suppose that as a nation we lost our oil, our energy resources, our trade. Even if these catastrophes were to occur each one of us would still possess something that economic crises or governments could never take away. Our skills and abilities will forever remain our own, they can only be shared.

In today's world the business of sharing and instructing skills becomes more important by the hour. A convincing argument is often advanced that our national, or even global, survival may depend on our using our own resources and abilities far better than we have in the past. What this means is that we have to learn to communicate our skills more efficiently to one another, to instruct in more effective ways and even to be prepared to instruct and to learn in settings undreamt of before.

The lay-out of our senses for instruction

When we instruct or teach an activity to someone we are at once engaged in one of the most easy and natural activities known to humans. And yet we so often overlook just how perfectly designed we are to give instruction. Imagine you are demonstrating a skill or activity to someone standing near you. Consider the lay-out of our limbs, hands, mouths, ears and eyes.

As you demonstrate both you and the learner can easily see what is taking place, for it is easy and convenient for us to work with our hands in full view of all. By having our mouths placed on the front of our faces we are able to demonstrate something with our hands whilst at the same time we can explain what we are doing to the onlooker standing before us. Likewise, we can readily talk to or ask questions of our onlooker because our eyes and ears face forward. As we are giving instruction we can, in a fraction of a second, raise our eyes from looking at what our hands are doing to see clearly the face of our inquisitive onlooker. We can instantly register his reactions, anticipate his questions, read his face.

Instruction is fun

There is one example of instruction which never fails to give anyone pleasure to watch and this is when young children undertake it. You must have noticed that children quite spontaneously will explain, will instruct, without any inhibitions whatsoever. They will do it to any interested onlooker or passer-by. Who of us has not at some time or other played at being the befuddled father or adult just in order to have youngsters explain and instruct? Just for the sheer fun of having children explain their tricks, games or puzzles we often get them to repeat again and again the simple instructions. We know full well that they are incredulous at our stupidity, but nevertheless we carry on asking for more explanations, more instructions. Why should this be so? One reason must be that we get pleasure from their totally carefree attitude to instruction. Here we are seeing a basic human activity undertaken just for the fun of it.

If we look closely at groups of young children gathering in playgrounds, alleyways or parks we will always see and hear an immense volume of serious practical instruction taking place. Instruction is spoken, shouted, screamed; instruction is whispered in corners — it is all a densely-woven network which covers the whole of a child's world. Instruction, along with play and make-believe, is part of the very fabric of childhood.

Children's faith in instruction

But what are the underlying attitudes of children towards instruction and towards sharing skills? It can help us, as adult instructors, to examine these. Children believe that anything can be explained, that anything can be learned; any craft, activity, sport or dodge is within reach of anyone. There is absolute faith in showing skills, in being able to give successful instruction. There is a total belief that any skill can be given from one person to another, simply by the process of instruction.

'Come on, join us, it's easy to do it. Look, watch me!'
'Here, I'll show you how to do it.'

Just listening to the urgency and conviction in children's voices as they explain to one another begins to make it easy for us to see how so many skills are successfully passed from one youngster to another.

Yet as adults we need not be smug and superior and claim that childhood skills are for the most part simple and easily learnt. They are often quite complicated, requiring careful instruction, tuition and demonstration. Watch youngsters showing each other how to manoeuvre on a skateboard, play a complicated street game or adjust the gearchange on a cycle and you will see. It is their attitude that is all-important here. It is an attitude of utter conviction, that instruction has got to work, cannot possibly fail, that sharing skills and learning is natural and easy. This attitude never fails to ring through in the voices of these young teachers.

Adults' instructing skills: what happens

This natural optimism and faith in instruction is not found so easily in adults. Especially, that is, if the adults are untrained as instructors and teachers. All too often the lay person called upon to instruct or demonstrate some activity feels somehow that he is no match for the task. Of course there will be exceptions, but generally speaking we find that the amateur or untrained instructor will become a little worried.

What happens? He begins to wonder if he is demonstrating the skill the correct way, or if he is using the right technique, or if he is explaining correctly. In short, sad though it sounds,

11

he has lost faith in his natural ability to instruct. But why should this be so?

Adult skills

A moment's reflection will reveal that it is not simply that the skills we have as adults have become too complicated to pass easily from one person to another. Hundreds of common household repair or construction skills, for instance, are not different in any great measure from childhood skills. We will look at this further when we examine skills in Chapter 3. Instead, as adults, we begin to believe that instruction can only be properly carried out by a person specially trained for the job: a qualified teacher, tutor, coach or trainer.

How many times have I heard perfectly capable people say things like:

> 'Even if I regard myself as a bit of an expert, I cannot
> teach you, I'm not qualified to, I wouldn't know how to
> start.'

Or, perhaps more common:

> 'Oh dear, I feel sure a proper teacher wouldn't demon-
> strate if the way I'm doing it.'

Skills as private property

If we begin to probe a little deeper we find that there is a change in how we view our skills the further we get away from childhood. Away from youth and childhood our skills increasingly come to be seen as our own personal property, our own private possessions. If other people want to learn them then we feel that they ought to enrol in classes to do so. We assume that they ought to make the sacrifice of study time or payment for tuition just as we did. Why on earth, we think, should we squander our hard-earned skills on other people? The skills cost us time and effort after all! In short, the innocent childhood willingness to share and explain has passed.

But not quite, for let us look at how and where instruction takes place among adults.

Two environments for instruction

Instruction in the form that we all have had most experience of takes place in buildings and institutions designed for that purpose. In colleges, in skill centres, in training establishments, in private tuition, in sports coaching clubs, and so on.

Restricted access

Common to all these examples is the fact that access to instruction is restricted. It is restricted to people who have the necessary entrance qualifications for college, university or polytechnic; who have paid their fees to join the sports coaching club; or who have paid large sums of money for private individual tuition.

Instruction usually takes place at set times of the day in surroundings which generally exclude outsiders from dropping in 'off the street' and benefiting. This type of environment we shall call 'restricted access.'

Open access

There are, however, other environments, often overlooked, where equally important practical instruction can be found taking place. Consider some examples:

☐ Motorists showing each other car maintenance or engine repair skills.
☐ Neighbours or allotment holders showing each other gardening skills and tips.
☐ Household/craft/survival/skills taught by parents to children (or vice versa!), or among friends and acquaintances.
☐ Young people showing each other the techniques of musical instrument playing.

We find in all these examples (and we can all find many more) that the person doing the instructing is unqualified. He is an amateur, 'one shot' instructor perhaps only infrequently called upon to demonstrate his skill. The person receiving the instruction has not usually paid any money as an entrance fee for instruction and is not required to possess any prior formal entrance qualifications. The exchange of skill requires only a willingness to instruct and a willingness to learn.

13

This type of environment we shall call 'open access' and it now deserves closer examination.

Because this type of instruction involves people getting together to learn and to instruct essentially in their own time, this does not rule out the possibility of there being a loose framework to organize this activity.

For example just recently some people decided to compile a simple card index among whoever was interested. The scheme was simple yet it was to prove a huge success.

They each wrote their names on a card and listed the practical skills, trades or crafts that they knew and were prepared to instruct. They included the times they would be available so that potential learners could contact them. The idea was that if you showed someone a skill you were entitled to learn another skill from someone else; likewise learning a skill put you under obligation to return some instruction to whoever might be interested.

The card index quickly grew; a large room was hired within easy reach of all, and a sign 'Skill Exchange' was pinned to the door. Eventually the participants came to study the index.

Soon there was a hive of activity with people instructing one another in all manner of skills, the floor quickly becoming strewn with tools, apparatus and equipment. In one corner a woman had an antique sofa in pieces on the floor before her: springs, stuffing, webbing, upholstery and tools lay around. Her learner was totally engrossed as the intricacies involved in renovating and re-upholstering old furniture were being explained. In another corner there was an island of intense concentration: two people were huddled together in the process of repairing a radio receiver. Next to them a girl, herself trained as a heating engineer, was demonstrating the soldering of complicated copper pipework joints. Her learner, it transpired, was determined to learn elementary plumbing skills in order to install his own solar heating system.

And so it went on. The overall impression of the activities in the room was one of genuine communication between people. The quiet murmur of instruction and conversation would occasionally be punctuated by hammering, the whine of power tools, or the clatter of hand tools. Or there would be the occasional peal of laughter or excitement as people discovered how easy it was to learn.

On leaving the room you realized that the 'Skill Exchange' had spilled out into the street and adjacent park. Car bonnets were raised, vehicles were jacked up, motor-bike engines were partly dismantled. On the field various sports were being demonstrated by the amateur coaches.

All this activity was taking place, almost without exception, among individuals who had never had the benefit of formal training in instructing or teaching skills. They had simply acquired their skill through the usual courses, trade training, 'teach yourself' books or were self-taught. What they lacked in teaching technique they made up for in enthusiasm, for each of the participants shared a determination to see the system grow. And grow it did.

Over a period of time a league table of popular skills was drawn up. Topping the list were joinery and furniture making, engine tuning, hair-cutting, hand-loom weaving, repairs to high fidelity sound equipment, yoga and relaxation exercises, guitar playing.

You came away from the whole endeavour with the feeling that here were great possibilities, that here was the unleashing of tremendous natural talent. Skills, hobbies, crafts — all were being taught by amateurs in a totally free learning environment with the minimum of bureaucratic control. There were no restrictions whatsoever on being able to learn, no previous certificates were needed, there were no age limits working against the not-so-young, no subtle forms of discrimination in operation.

OTHER EXAMPLES OF OPEN ACCESS LEARNING

Overseas examples of open access instruction ranging from university studies to survival agricultural skills are described elsewhere (Illich 1971, 1973, McKenzie *et al.* 1975, Holt 1977). Some experiences of setting up open access learning systems in Britain for instructors and academic staff have been described elsewhere by the author (Winfield 1975, 1977, 1984, 1986).

Variation in instruction success

It is clear that both restricted access and open access instruction can vary in important ways. As we all know, instruction, wherever it takes place, and under whatever circumstances, can be either successful or unsuccessful. It can be efficient and with a high level of skill transfer from instructor to learner. Or at the other extreme it can be sloppy and inefficient. This is the kind of instruction that is a hit-and-miss affair with consequently a high failure rate among learners.

How the two extremes differ

These two extremes of successful and unsuccessful instruction differ in one important way. This is simply in the amount of respect they each have for the way people actually learn and in the use made of the psychology of learning and instruction.

We all know of examples of hopeless instruction, based essentially on the hunch or intuition of the instructor. The instructor here invariably has no time for psychology or theories of how people learn. Instruction is a case of just brutally bumbling on.

On the other hand we find that successful instructors will actively use many of the well-tried principles of instruction.

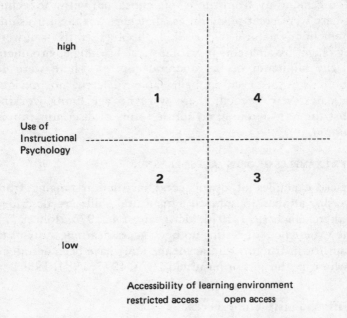

Figure 1. *The relationship between instructional psychology and accessibility of learning*

Instruction here is clear, precise and systematic — and it gets the results intended.

In Figure 1 the vertical axis shows the differing use of the psychology of learning and instruction: as noted, it can either be high or low use. The horizontal axis shows the two types of access to learning as mentioned earlier.

We can now examine the four resulting situations.

1. *High use of instructional psychology but restricted access*

Examples would include:

- ☐ Advanced industrial training courses.
- ☐ Forces training.
- ☐ Tuition in further/higher education.

We find here training courses using highly selected and highly trained personnel. These instructors have been taught, often at great expense, how to design and give first-rate instruction. They all make great use daily of the psychology of learning in order to make their instruction effective, and are always ready to employ different instructional tactics. Often, but not always, they are backed up in their work by developments in educational technology: they can, if necessary, use training films, film loops, video cameras and tapes, computer assisted instruction. It remains a pity that more learners cannot benefit from this type of instruction.

2. *Low uses of instructional psychology but restricted access*

Examples might be:

- ☐ Outdated and inefficient industrial training schemes.
- ☐ Inefficient private coaching.

In this situation we still have restricted access but instruction would be inefficient and slipshod. Training schemes in firms would have abysmally high failure rates among trainees, with poor quality results. In the case of poor private paid coaching, be it sports, language, music or driving, it is doubtful whether the coaches would be able to stay in business for long, consistently showing such poor results. The sad thing is that they do.

3. *Open access/low use of instructional psychology*

Our previous examples of neighbours or friends sharing skills, as well as our 'Skill Exchange' example, fall into this category. It is open access in that any interested parties can join, but unfortunately it is low in its use of the psychology of learning and instruction. The truth has to be faced. Although these open access examples are interesting and often exciting ventures, instruction in these circumstances is often woefully inadequate. The failure rate in the 'Skill Exchange' venture was fairly high; people often dropped out, unable to get their particular skill across. Either that or they were unable to learn from others. And this happens all the time, not just in specially arranged skill exchanges. A shrug of the shoulders, a despairing 'Oh I give up', and all is lost.

Yet this is only because people fail to use even the minimum of common-sense psychology. All they need to help them on the road to successful instruction are a few sound guiding principles.

4. *The scope and challenge: open access/high use of instructional psychology*

One of the most pressing problems that we face today is making more effective use of our resources. We need to be prepared to instruct and to learn in totally new situations. We need to communicate and share our skills across outdated age barriers, to communicate and share skills held previously to be the domain of one sex only.

Each one of us is quite capable of turning into an effective instructor and sharer of skills. To show, to share, to explain — these are the activities we should be undertaking.

In conclusion there is no mystique about instruction. There is no special touch, inborn ability or art to successful instruction. Just as we pick up a do-it-yourself manual and promptly have a go at doing any job ourselves, so it ought to be with instruction. We can teach ourselves to be effective instructors. The principles and rules are here to be learnt and used.

References

Holt, J (1977) *Instead of Education: Ways to help people do things better*. Penguin, London.

Illich, I D (1971) *Deschooling Society*. Calder & Boyars, London.

Illich, I D (1973) *Tools for Conviviality*. Calder & Boyars, London.

McKenzie, N Postgate, R and Scupham J (1975) *Open Learning: Systems and Problems in Post Secondary Education*. UNESCO, Paris.

Winfield, I J and Dallos, R (1975) Instructional Strategies in Industrial Training and Rehabilitation. *Journal of Occupational Psychology*, 48, 4, 241-252.

Winfield, I J (1977) Staff Resources and Innovation: Open Learning for Polytechnic teachers. *Aspects of Educational Technology XI*. In Hills, P & Gilbert, J (eds) Kogan Page, London.

Winfield, I J (1984) *People in Business*. Heinemann, London.

Winfield I J (1986) *Human Resources and Computing*. Heinemann, London.

Chapter 2
Making contact

Overview: This second chapter looks at how to make effective
social contact with the person you intend to instruct. A good
relationship based on mutual understanding and respect between
instructor and learner will always be the basis for successful
instruction. Successful relationships do not happen by chance; they
have to be created and worked upon. This is particularly so in skill
instruction today where barriers of age, sex and ethnic divide are
increasingly being crossed.

Established role relationships

The instructor and trainee are together engaged in what is
called an 'established role relationship'. To understand what
this means and the demands it makes on both parties let us
examine some other established role relationships in practice.
Within established role relationships people's behaviour is
expected to follow more or less set patterns in order to facil-
itate the easy reaching of some specified goal. Consider as
illustrations the everyday occurrence of paying for something
we wish to purchase, be it petrol at a self-service garage, goods
bought in a shop, or a ticket from a conductor. First you,
the potential buyer, proffer the goods or declare what it is
you have purchased. The vendor checks the details and you
tender the money or payment. This is accepted and change
(with or without a receipt) is given. Finally, thanks are usually
exchanged.

What is it that makes this transaction usually work so well?
The smoothness emanates from both parties being essentially
skilled players of their roles: both know what the other's
needs are. They both know without prompting when it is their
turn to act in the 'mini-drama'.

Countless times during each day mini-dramas such as these
are played. For people employed in jobs with a high incidence
of social contact (retail employment is a good example) such
short, established role relationships constitute the whole of
their working lives. Professional bliss for them is when all
contact runs smoothly and predictably — people have the right
change, know exactly what they want, do not query the
receipt and so on.

Accept, if you will, that an instructional sequence is simply an example of an established role relationship. Now, if we analyse in a little more depth the simplest form of established role relationship (taking the buying example quoted earlier) then we will have the key to understanding some useful truths about instruction. It is for the instructor's fundamental benefit that there are common elements. And since we all know intuitively what is required in simple established role relationships, both teacher and learner also know what to do in instruction. This is especially true for the trainee, who will arrive at the first instructional session already programmed to behave in a certain way. Their expectations are high — they are expecting an established role relationship complete with its unspoken rules, even though they might not recognise it as such. So just what is it that they consciously expect?

Instruction as transaction

During instruction something is given, something received. Trainees are expecting a purchase. Above all it is a trans-action where you, the instructor, are expected to have the upper hand. You must acknowledge this. You are expected to have the upper hand, not just for wielding authority or exploiting your position. You must be the initiator. The learner wants you to subtly control things to their best learning advantage.

This quality of leadership is known as directiveness and it is always a sound policy for the novice instructor to accept it, acknowledge and use it when necessary, in early interactions with the learner. Knowing your own practical skill inside out is fine, but it is not enough to make you an inspired first-rate instructor. You should now appreciate that the delivery of that skill, the style and manner in which it is presented, in the opening stages, is uppermost in the mind of the learner. You then, are expected to make the running, firmly yet sympathetically. Commitment to making the transaction, not just the skill is therefore important. The skill can never speak for itself — it is dumb. It cannot fire enthusiasm, it is the instructor who brings it alive. It is you as director, producer and chief performer in the drama who is going to make it all happen.

Turn-taking in instruction

Crucial to the smooth, efficient running of any established role relationship, be it short and sharp like buying, or long and complicated like instruction, is the phenomenon of turn-taking. Unless both parties recognize that the action takes place first in one partner then in the other, then nothing could ever take place, nothing would be exchanged. Like enjoyable conversation, instruction is characterised by polite bursts of speaking and listening. You cannot speak and listen at the same time. Remind people of this if necessary — it is acceptable to do so. The learner is unconsciously expecting this. He will anticipate and be ready for these short bursts of activity and inactivity. Speaking and listening, looking and doing, listening and asking questions. He will expect you to provide periods in which he can talk or ask questions. He will expect to have to pay close attention to what is said or demonstrated while waiting to perform and perhaps ask questions.

Silence followed by speech, inaction followed by demonstration, trial followed by performance — all this demonstrates the essential periodicity of effective instruction. Working in your favour is the mental set of expectations of your trainee. He requires you, and no one else, to set the pace, tone and emotional atmosphere of the session. You are expected to schedule the training session — they for their part must be keen, attendant listeners and to be observant. It is a two-way transaction, a balance. I have known highly successful instructors who consciously 'play-up' to the turn-taking element in a gentle, bantering sort of way. Likewise I have seen instructors start the session hopelessly and on the wrong foot by simply neglecting to establish the turn-taking element. One instructor in a health centre 'programmes' her groups extremely well using the following trick. The first introductory session begins with everyone milling around together, taking coffee, meeting fellow participants. After ten minutes or so she raises her voice above the background noise and says 'Can I just have your attention for a few seconds?' Conversation stops. 'My turn for just a minute.' She continues:

'My name is Anne and I will be giving the first session. I shall be giving an introductory talk and will sketch out the evening's programme when we've finished coffee. We start next door in about five minutes time. Carry on — there's more coffee left if you need it.'

An instructor in motor vehicle maintenance and repair uses another similar technique.

'So that's how that section is done. Any questions. No? Yes? Right, your turn now. Come on off your backsides, my turn to sit down. Come on, up you get.'

To a very large extent the instructor derives the rules for turn-taking. It is difficult to legislate and make recommendations for all skills here, for the nature of the skill will dictate the form and frequency of turn-taking. If the skill is physically demanding or dangerous then naturally you will want people to take their turn and ask questions when you think it is fit and safe to do so. Let the learners know this, let them know that questions or requests for repeats have to come when you are ready for them. It is easy to do this simply by asking them to save all their requests up until the end. The real trick is to get your learners conditioned into accepting the turn-taking game yet not to let them feel that it is inhibiting their spontaneity and enjoyment in any way. A few trials and experiments will quickly establish the particular method best suited to your skill.

Selling yourself

We live in a society dominated by the growth in retailing. The act of purchase is increasingly regarded as a social occasion for all the family, not without its own inherent pleasures. Witness the creation of shopping malls, covered shopping plazas, supermarkets with recreation and refreshment facilities. This is a sign of the times and, strange though it may seem it can be advantageous for you the skill instructor. People just adore being sold something. They love the attention, the action, the uncertainty and tension surrounding the decision whether to buy or to leave well alone. To them it is their very own daily drama. They, and no one else, are centre stage — the spotlight is on them.

Believing that you are selling both yourself and the skill can get you in the correct frame of mind for making contact and beginning instruction. Like any sales person you are an ambassador. To succeed you have to put your best foot forward, and you have to do some soul-searching to find out what in fact this is. Skilled, successful sales people have been trained to undertake what are known as 'vendor ploys'. These are strategies that help the sales process progress and gently nudge the sale along to a successful closure. The ploys in current use are many, but notable among them are direct eye contact with the customer, smiling at them, agreeing or reinforcing what the potential customer says (a variant on the 'customer is always right' homily).

The novice instructor is well advised to seek out and experiment with his own personal set of 'ploys' in this way. How best do you seem to sell yourself? What seems to work best when making contact? What method is most effective with this particular group of people? Is it jokes, a particular line of banter, a story? When we study 'training failures' — trainees who have abandoned courses of instruction — we find the simple truth that trainees buy not the skill itself but the person who is or was trying to instruct them. They often report that they could not get on with the instructor, that the instructor was unable to motivate them, that they did not like them as people. There is nothing new in these findings. Children's chosen school subject, in which they may excel reveals a fascination just as much with the teacher as with the particular subject. An effective instructor, just like an inspired teacher, must learn to transform the dullest of subjects into a glittering challenge.

I was once evaluating a course on techniques of instruction. The course organisers had recruited an outside guest instructor to start off the first session. The particular instructor was chosen as a role model because it was felt he was particularly good at 'selling himself' and presenting skills in an interesting and challenging way. He chose to start the session off by first demonstrating Origami, the ancient Japanese art of paper folding. He was able to transform a rudimentary paper-folding exercise by a combination of bewitching, running dialogue, jokes and gentle teasing into a real intellectual challenge, so much so that the spellbound trainees were literally itching to start. The task was mundane: the performance brilliant. Reflecting on the success of the introductory session I have to conclude that it was not 'charisma' or personality factors or even something metaphysical like being a 'gifted' teacher that contributed to his outstanding success. Instead it was a carefully studied and rehearsed performance honed to perfection. The instructor had in fact laboriously studied people's reactions to different ways of presenting the paper folding exercise.

He had in the past experimented countless times with different strategies. At the course debriefing session he told me candidly that he had tried countless ways of getting the skill across — some were successful, others outright failures. He had tried new ploys, varied old routines, mixed the old with the new.

But in his eyes, a selling act it was and remained. That single concept was his guiding idea throughout. It was the one notion that drove him to seek perfection in presentation. And it worked admirably. After one demonstration you were irremediably hooked, for you just could not wait to 'pay your money' and have a go at the skill.

Getting to know people

When we meet people we always underestimate the power of first impressions. Although intuition may tell us not to be fooled by first impressions and that first appearances can be deceptive, we are all nevertheless seduced by the first few moments of interaction with strangers. In these first few critical moments both partners to the meeting will be positively bombarded with impressions of the other. They will ask themselves all manner of questions. Questions such as 'Am I going to like this person?' 'Do I find it pleasant to be with this person?' Each person will try and establish background facts like age, social class and other variables. It is a process we all undertake and it would be dishonest to claim that we do not do it. Rarely, though, do we stop to analyse the process but if we could we would find instant, snap decisions being taken.

Skilled instructors are well aware of this. They know that they must stage first meetings correctly. They know that they have to arrange things to their best advantage. Often they carefully arrange the setting for the first encounter. They consider the setting, the environment, the context, of that first crucial meeting. They ensure there are not interruptions, they complete outstanding work or projects so that they can give the new trainees their total, undivided attention. This fact, more than any other, contributes to getting the relationship off on the right foot.

On one occasion I asked a learner how she felt about her instructor after he had just given an introductory session. 'There was something I just could not put my finger on,' she mused. 'Right from the word go there was something about the instructor's whole attitude and bearing that, well, just was not right somehow. As if he was only half there, as if he wasn't really interested in us mere learners. It seemed as if he had done it so many times, he was only going through the motions. I felt that there was something happening in the background — off-stage as it were, perhaps in his family life or something — such that he did not really want to be there with us.'

Such perceptiveness in novice learners is by no means unusual — it is living testimony to the heightened awareness people have during early interactions.

I later talked to the instructor in question 'That opening session was ghastly', he said. 'Positively everything went wrong. The video cassette recorder was playing up. I had left it until the very last moment before the session before checking it over. With it not working correctly that meant I had to quickly think of alternative things for the learners to do. I had too much on my mind — and I knew it.'

This example illustrates two things. First, it shows vividly that adequate preparation should always precede your first meeting with trainees. These points are considered more fully in the next chapter. Second, it illustrates that for the crucial first contact with learners the social aspects of your presentation are foremost. A calm, collected approach can and will allow the instructor to concentrate on the positive aspects of his personality and performance. Only when everything is under control and adequately prepared can the instructor give of his best. The issues of self projection in the initial few minutes are what we shall turn to next, for there are certain aspects of our personality and presentation that we need to 'work on' so that they are effectively conveyed to the trainees.

Using first impressions to your advantage

All people, when they meet others, exhibit stable, regular ways of forming first impressions. Humans, as has been said countless times before, are creatures of habit. Common habitual ways of forming first impressions has been the subject of a considerable amount of recent research which can be used beneficially (Adams-Webber 1979).

An initial encounter with an instructor is seen by the trainee as an opportunity for testing a few suppositions or hypotheses.

27

'Just what is this person like?' 'Is this instruction going to be too difficult for me, am I going to be able to cope?' Questions such as these are prominent in the minds of learners. Our advice to instructors is: try and project a warm, understanding and sympathetic aspect of yourself. It is there within you, waiting to come out, to be released by the right opportunities. Now is the time to cultivate these qualities.

When you ask learners what sorts of thoughts and feelings they have when they first meet their instructor, remarkable similarities begin to emerge. Try it sometime, it can be wonderfully informative and instructive.

'I am usually slow at picking things up, I wonder if the instructor will understand?'
'I do hope this instructor isn't deadly serious and lacking in humour — I find that so off putting.'

What do comments such as these really reveal? All of them express a deep-seated need for the instructor to be human, warm and kind. Human in that they will be sympathetic to ordinary failings and struggles and warm in that they can readily project a caring attitude, showing basic civility and kindness.

A good tip for openings or introductions is always to open with something that is immediately on the arriving trainee's mind. This indicates that you care, that you sense their requirements, even before you start the session.

Did they find the venue satisfactorily? No wrong turnings or misdirections? Were there traffic or transport difficulties? Are all of their responsibilities taken care of? These are some of the questions to ask. There are countless ways instructors engineer successful first meetings with people. Undoubtedly these are ploys, and the ploys used may be as contrived and well-tried as the vendor ploys used by your average door-to-door sales person, but nevertheless they work.

Another useful tip for introductory meetings is to remember that you, the instructor will have plenty of time to talk and hear your own voice later. Force yourself to take a back seat to start with; for getting the trainee to talk and open up never fails. Irrespective of whether you are instructing a small group or tutoring individual learners this is always a good way of dispelling 'first time' nerves. Choose conversation topics that you find they are confident about, that they feel at home with or are themselves expert at. There has to be something. Perhaps topics that you find are emotionally close to them (but not threateningly so) such as their background, family, children or holidays. These topics can exist as a stable bedrock for future interactions, for there is one thing they, as learners, are certain about. They may be absolute idiots at learning a skill but at least they are certain about their own likes and dislikes, their jobs, their hopes for the future. Find subjects which will let them become expansive, hear themselves expounding on what they firmly know. The great launch into the unknown is to follow later!

Research on people getting to know one another (Argyle, Henderson 1983) reveals a process which we call self disclosure. Self disclosure is the systematic revealing of aspects of the self to another person and it follows its own well charted course of events. Fortunately we can turn this to effective use in instruction. What happens when people meet is that first one person will 'test the water' by revealing some aspect of their self or social life, their likes and dislikes, preferences and so on — parts of life normally hidden from casual social contacts. If the relationship shows promise of developing further then the other person will probably reciprocate: perhaps revealing tentatively some aspect of their private life or aspect of self. The two people then proceed, if all goes well, to uncover aspects of themselves at a mutually regulated pace. Satisfactory relationships seem to occur most frequently when people do not reveal themselves too quickly thus causing embarrassment. Above all, those skilled in making contact show sensitivity to this rate of disclosure. They 'mesh' smoothly with the acceptable rate of exchange — allowing the unfolding of the relationship and the process of getting to know the other person to proceed without hitches.

Instructors will often be starting a relationship with their learners which will of necessity involve the steady building of a sound relationship; a relationship built on trust and acceptance. The old idea of the expert or sage who is neutral, remote or aloof is no longer applicable in today's changing world. It is not enough, just being an excellent craftsperson or skilled instructor. People simply dislike aloofness in teachers. You must show yourself to be human, essentially by reciprocating keenly when social contact is offered.

Do not try and be some sort of neuter, devoid of gender or

social background and experience. Match social contact and self revelation with the same. What preferences do you have in common? Do you have any shared experiences or background? Any views on current events? Creating social space together rests on the willingness to test, to offer others aspects of yourself and to venture a little vulnerability to life's knocks.

Crossing barriers

An increasing amount of practical skills instruction is taking place in a multicultural environment. The cultural, sexual, age and ethnic divide is being crossed more often. This is a development to be applauded — not just because of the democratic payoffs of a broadened skill base, but also because the task of instruction itself becomes infinitely more challenging and rewarding. Let us now examine some specific techniques of crossing various types of 'divides'.

It may come as a truism to many, but it is easiest for us to communicate with members of our own class, education and social background. This is not to say that divides are not crossed successfully. They are, admirably well. But special effort, particularly on the part of the instructor, has to be made. Everyone has preconceptions regarding people who are different in some way from themselves. These preconceptions have to be consciously worked through. Is our stereotyping negative or derogatory in any way? Has it been manufactured by the tabloid press? Who are the current 'folk devils' in the public eye, created by a stereotyping and sensationalist media?

The most important question is: can we allow our experience, here and now with this person, to change our prejudices and stereotypes — and are we willing to let this happen?

One instructor I knew had the immensely difficult task of instructing a class from widely differing backgrounds. Learners were from different cultural backgrounds; some were young, some were old, many were people 'just passing through' the inner-city area where the instruction was taking place. There were cases of deprivation and poverty, there were people of relative affluence. How did the instructor begin to communicate with persons of such radically different lifestyles? This instructor explains:

'There is one guiding principle I always try and follow. For me in particular it goes right back to my college days. The philosopher Jean-Paul Sartre once said "existence precedes essence". This is one of the guiding tenets of the philosophy called existentialism. There is nothing highbrow or abstract about this, like many people are led to believe. For me it simply means that each person is unique. Unique that is, no matter what label, colour, race, creed or sex. I just wipe everything out about past experiences, get a 'clean slate' as it were, and start with the person — from square one. As they are. As they stand before me. First I level with them. I get to know them. Get the 'feel' of them as I call it. This for me is the one most important thing in the early sessions. There might be 10 or 20 people in my charge, but I always make enough social space to meet each person on a one-to-one basis. Not social chit-chat or mindless patter, but trying to find out about their backgrounds, where their heads are at, why they want to learn. All the time, of course, I know I will be meeting them again the following week so I deliberately make what I call a 'trailer' for each person. That is usually some topic or other that we've been chatting about together. I make this into perhaps an ongoing topic to pick up at the next meeting. It keeps the same social scene going. When I first started instructing people I used to make little notes about each new trainee. It served as a simple memory aid. Now I don't bother anymore, for if I can remember just one or two 'trailers' for each person, I can carry it on from week to week. It makes barriers just that much easier to surmount.'

The value of understanding people's constructs

A construct system is a set of ideas we have about something or somebody. We usually find that constructs hang together in clearly defined ways. Stereotyping is the best known example of the way constructs hold firmly together.

Stereotyping follows the kind of reasoning which says 'all X's are invariably Y's'. Now, everybody knows that stereotyping people is somehow wrong, but we do it nevertheless. Trainees do it, anyone about to learn a skill does it and so does anyone about to be taught. It can take many forms but some of the more common stereotypes of instructors that learners have are as follows. 'All instructors are talkative.' 'Instructors are failed crafts people.' Instructors also have stereotypes of

31

learners, for example: 'All so-and-so's are lazy and will not learn'.

Research shows that in initial encounters we are continually testing the validity of these ideas. We are testing the adequacy of our own construction of the other person (Duck 1973, 1986).

The important point for us to note is that understanding other peoples' constructs is the key to managing our relationship with them. This means asking specific questions. It means reaching out and trying to get into the construct systems existing in the head of the learner. The instructor should ask: 'Just why does this learner have such low expectations of instruction? Have they tried in the past and failed? What were the circumstances then? How and why are things different now?'

The instructor has to do some soul-searching and self analysis too. For example why is it that you, the instructor, expect so little of this particular learner? Is it possibly because you see them as one of a particular type? A type, class or creed you have had negative experiences with before? Can you break out of this thinking; will you let yourself break free from the past?

Only rigorous self-examination and continually questioning the basis of our assumptions can help us overcome rigidity of constructs. Reaching a person's core, getting to know his value system and respecting it for what it is (irrespective of whether we agree with it or not) is undoubtedly hard work. Essentially it means rolling up your mental sleeves and moving beyond superficial social banter. It means moving beyond the ritualized and banal 'Hi – have a nice day' exchange. It means levelling with the other person, talking person-to-person with them. Talking, not as a representative of a skill or an organization to a stereotyped learner, but as an individual to an individual – finding out and trying to understand.

Conclusion

Some reference has been made in this chapter to the cash nexus in society. True, most skills are learnt simply for monetary gain – or the hope of it. To get a better 'toehold' in the labour market for skills is undoubtedly the underlying motivation for vocational skill learning. Money, not the skill itself, is the real reason why instructor and trainee are brought together.

But generalizations like these dismiss all other reasons. People are complex, they are driven by multiple and inter-acting motives. Crude blanket statements like 'We are are all driven simply by the desire for money' belie the deeper, more subtle and interesting reasons.

Of course, to an extent, all learning is for monetary gain, but skill learning has other advantages as well. For the person who wants to learn a new skill, learning it is somehow a means of making a connection. People see the skill as a means of establishing contact. The new skill will render them more contemporary. It will open doors to the future and offer hope. Hope of personal growth, of becoming more whole, of perhaps becoming more in tune with individual abilities and true selves. The skill thus represents a reaching out and as such can be seen as a birth of something new for the future. If we can begin to touch this level of deeper meaning in people's choice we are well on the road to making contact — and enjoying it.

References

Adams-Webber, J R (1979) *Personal Construct Theory: Concepts and Applications*. Wiley, London.

Argyle, M and Henderson, M (1983) *Rules of Relationships*. Heinemann, London.

Duck, S (1973) *Personal Relationships and Personal Constructs: a study of friendship formation*. Wiley, London.

Duck, S (1986) *Human Relationships*. Sage, London.

Chapter 3
The nature of our everyday skills

Overview: In this chapter the question is posed: 'what is the nature of the apparatus in our bodies and brains that allows us to exercise skill in various tasks?'

This question is answered by looking at a simple information processing model of human skilled performance. This model allows us to understand better the nature of everyday skills; to analyse what lies beind the phrase 'there's a knack in it'.

Understanding what is involved in skills puts us on the first step to becoming a better instructor.

What is a skill?

We all agree that tradespeople, surgeons, actors, homemakers, mothers and toddlers all show skills in some way or other. We know also that when we say some behaviour is 'skilled' it will strike us as more or less complex and that it will have to be learned. Dictionary definitions of the word 'skill' give us the following:

— practical knowledge in combination with ability; cleverness, expertness.

— to have discrimination or knowledge especially in a specified matter.

— reason as a faculty of mind; the power of discrimination.

(Oxford English Dictionary)

But dictionary definitions only tell us how we use words in an everyday setting. For the purposes of becoming better instructors we need to know more about the psychological meaning of skill. We need a definition which tells us something about what it means to have a skill, and how we can begin to instruct in a skill. Study the following phrases:

A skill is any series of mental or physical acts executed in such a way as to demonstrate complete control by the executor.

Complete control depends on the building up of co-ordinated activity involving different senses, our mental abilities and our muscles.

Skills are learnt by building from experience and practice.

35

Skills involve a series of behaviours arranged carefully in time.

(Adapted from Welford 1968)

All the phrases suggest valuable aspects of skill, though the idea we will explore is contained in the phrase 'co-ordinated activity involving different senses, our mental abilities and our muscles'. This tells us there are three vital parts to a skill and it brings us to the model of skill used throughout this book.

The information processing model of skill

A model is simply a rough map or guide to help us understand. It should not be taken literally or be expected to exist in any real sense. The real value of our model of skill which we are about to examine is that it allows us to classify, describe and understand even the most complex of skills. To instruct successfully we must first be able to do this.

An example

We begin by analysing a skill being demonstrated by you at this moment: reading.

Along with walking, talking and eating, reading is a skill we practise so frequently that we take it for granted. But what is reading skill? Can we find any different parts or components to the skill of reading? Can we understand it any better than we do already?

Reading, as we are all aware, is a complex activity. It is a skill that is both rapid and highly organized. Most important for us, though, is the fact that the skill of reading demonstrates the interrelationships of the four important elements of all skills. These are:

1. The input of information from our senses.
2. The brain planning and taking decisions.
3. The output of actions undertaken by limbs.
4. Feedback from the output to the input.

The first stage

Let us take these four parts in turn. At the moment the input to you, the reader, is light carrying visible patterns of this black print on this white page. This input of light itself carries no meaning. It is merely a black and white pattern seen by our eyes. This process is shown in Figure 2.

36

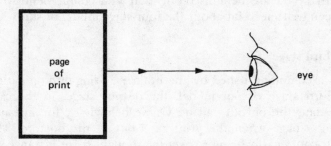

Figure 2. *The input stage*

Our understanding of the meaning of the letters, words and sentences printed on the page does not lie in the light patterns at all. The information is still just patterned light input and it passes through the eye to the light-sensitive retina at the back.

The second stage

Here, behind the eye in the retina the light is translated into electrical nervous impulses which are sent on their way to the second stage of our model of reading. This is shown in Figure 3.

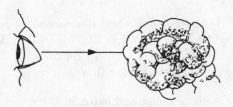

Figure 3. *The brain*

It is here in the brain that we begin to comprehend the meaning of the print; to understand what we have read printed on the page. Let us examine again what has happened so far. The eye, as the sense organ of the system, scans the text and supplies our brains with information. Here, in the second stage, decisions are made as to the intelligibility of what is read. It is

37

here that you are demonstrating that you comprehend what has been written so far about the four-stage model of skill.

The third stage

Upon a command issued by the brain we bring into operation the third stage of our model, the output stage. In the case of reading the output can be visible behaviour, for instance turning a page when the print runs out at the bottom. The output could easily be more exciting though. If for instance we are reading a guidebook we might easily rush off and explore for ourselves the places mentioned.

Yet the output from reading need not always be so noticeable. As a result of reading we might easily experience new insights, new ideas, even changed attitudes. The point is, whether the activity from reading is physical or purely mental, reading always has a definite output. This third stage of reading is illustrated in Figure 4.

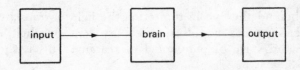

Figure 4. *Input — brain — output*

With the third stage described our model of reading skill is nearly complete. Except, that is, for the links that exist between the three stages. This can be illustrated by reading the instruction below and following it.

Now re-examine **Figure 3**. *The brain.*

To undertake this command is to switch backwards and forwards between the printed instruction and Figure 3 — re-reading the instruction, peering closely at the figure. In this case the physical output of actions by our fingers and our arms can alter the input. By turning the page back we can represent the input (Figure 3); by turning the page forward we can represent the command. This link between output stage and input stage is called the feedback loop. This loop completes the four-part model and is illustrated in Figure 5.

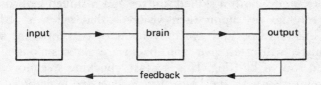

Figure 5. *Information processing model of skill*

This four-stage model we shall now use to examine skills other than reading. We start with stage one, the input stage.

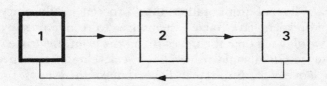

Stage 1: the input stage

Our senses supply the input to our system. The six senses used separately or in combination with one another are as follows:

- ☐ vision
- ☐ hearing
- ☐ touch
- ☐ smell
- ☐ taste
- ☐ proprioceptive sense (the sense which tells us the position of our limbs in space – crucial for many skills).

We shall examine only the three most used senses in skills – vision, hearing and touch.

We are so dependent upon these senses for supplying information to use about the world that we often overlook aspects of their working. For instance we invariably forget how particular senses can become highly developed and refined for use in skills. This is well illustrated in skills relying heavily on vision.

Vision

Vision is the most important sense by which information about the outside world reaches us. But when we move our eyes we often use our vision in surprisingly different ways.

39

For example, both a skilled knitter and a skilled embroiderer will rely heavily upon their vision — that much is obvious. But this is vision and eye movement of two different kinds. A knitter will often give rapid backward glances along a completed row of knitting. This is a fast 'checking' eye movement. Compare this with the kind of vision needed in embroidering. Here the person engages in careful methodical scrutinizing of the thread, using a steady careful gaze.

A type of eye movement and vision unlike the previous two examples is used by extremely rapid readers. Each time a reader's eyes fix on the print they do not move smoothly over a line of print, rather they proceed jerkily, unevenly. Rapid readers have trained themselves to read more surrounding words each time their eyes fix on the print. Evidence seems to suggest that rapid readers do not develop greater speed of eye movement, but rather have trained themselves to read more words at the edge of their visual 'cone' outside the point focused on.

SKILL INSTRUCTION: AN EXAMPLE USING VISION

A young mother was keen on embroidery. She was pestered by her youngest son (5) who wanted to learn the craft himself. Although he was not yet fully accomplished even at threading a needle, he was evidently keen to learn. The mother quickly realized too that although her son possessed the necessary eyesight, he had never attempted really close, fine-detailed vision tasks. She recognized that the sense-input was of a particularly developed form in embroidery — and so she decided to tutor her young son selectively in this ability.

She arranged a simple larger-than-life embroidery ring on which were placed threads. Threads, that is, not of fine, difficult-to-discriminate silk, but of thick, coloured, chunky wool. The child, mastering the principles of threading, was soon easily able to 'embroider' happily with thick wool. She then replaced the wool with thinner cord. Again she encouraged her son to practise. She replaced the cord with successively thinner string until finally she arrived at the authentic fine silk thread she commonly used, and which, of course, her young son insisted on using.

The child had been effectively 'trained' how to use fine-detailed vision for a simple skill by a method both playful and effective.

When instructing in skills which rely heavily on vision it can help you to ask the following questions:

TIPS FOR INSTRUCTION

☐ Is there any special kind of vision needed to perform the skill?

☐ In the early stages of the task can the learner clearly distinguish and understand the visual features of the task?

☐ Do you need to 'highlight', 'enlarge', or somehow exaggerate the principles to be learned?

☐ Is it worthwhile developing a simple training exercise, like our skill instruction example?

Hearing

Unlike our eyes, our ears do not possess lids. We cannot, except by using earplugs or fingers, totally close our ears. We cannot easily change the source of input in the way that we did earlier with our page of print. It is simple for you to obliterate this print by either shutting your eyes or looking up from the page. In each case the inputs change immediately, drastically.

Only, however, with mental effort can we switch between the sound inputs.

Try it. First try to isolate and attend to sounds coming from your immediate vicinity — for instance your own breathing, the slight rustle of your clothing or of furniture. Next listen selectively to more distant background sounds — traffic, aircraft, neighbours, or the wind. Essentially this has to be a conscious 'switching' process, or a kind of mental filtering... doesn't it? We generally have to think hard to be able to do it.

This fact is important for instructing in skills where hearing is involved. In vision if something critical goes unnoticed by the learner, an instructor can point it out, highlight or enlarge it. Not so with hearing. Very often the noise in question is always present. The problem is that the learner has not noticed it, he has not attended to something that has always been present.

GETTING THE LEARNER TO LISTEN CORRECTLY

The role of an instructor, then, is often to make the learner

41

aware of sounds, to teach him to be aware of the critical sound. Often it is sound embedded within background 'masking' noise. This is particularly true for diagnostic skills involving engines. Car engine noises provide a common example.

SKILL INSTRUCTION: AN EXAMPLE

A student was instructing a young teenage girl how to sand floorboards down to bare wood prior to treating. The hire and transport charge for the necessary power tool — an industrial drum sander — was beyond the means of the student, so he was limited to using his power drill with the sanding disc attachment. The job was slow but providing he didn't burn the motor out by overloading it was relatively cheap.

In instructing the young girl he drew her attention to the problem of overloading the motor, then let her start sanding her own room under his supervision. Repeatedly, she would press too hard, slowing the motor down — each time bringing pained expressions to the student's face. Finally, in exasperation he stopped her and asked her why she was repeatedly slowing the motor down.

'But I'm not slowing it down,' she said, 'I'm looking carefully and I can't see it slowing down at all.'

It was then he realized that the girl was attempting to use the wrong sense channel to undertake the simple task. His job then was to tell the girl what sense to use and to cue her into analysing the sound correctly: to teach her to discriminate successfully.

'Here, let me demonstrate. You see it's all done by hearing. Shut your eyes. Listen to the high "wheeee ..." of the motor when it's running free.' He demonstrated. 'Listen how the sound goes lower when it slows down,' and he demonstrated the overloaded, lowered pitch. 'As you sand the floor keep the drill singing really high; listen as I do it.'

After demonstrating a few strokes he handed her back the drill.

To instruct in skills relying on the use of hearing:

TIPS FOR INSTRUCTION

☐ Is it possible to start and stop the critical sound in order to get the learner to notice it? (For example try turning up the treble tone control to illustrate high frequency 'hiss' in a radio tuner, or accentuating bass to illustrate turntable 'rumble'.)

TIPS FOR INSTRUCTION *(continued)*

☐ If the learner is having trouble discriminating the sound from others (as in engine noises) try to mimic the sound yourself or try to find suitable similes which describe the sound.

Touch

Of all our senses it seems that touch communicates most immediately with our innermost selves. We speak of being 'gripped' with fear, of being 'moved' to tears, of being 'touched' by some moving scene.

Touch has another strange quality, particularly when people have to learn to develop touch in skills. It is as if touching is seen as somehow wrong. To meddle, to touch or to feel with our hands, always strikes us as somehow just a little indulgent. It is something we feel we ought to have grown out of as adults.

Thus it can be said that many of our rediscovered handcraft skills are pleasant, acceptable ways of enjoying publicly the pleasure of touch, of manipulating things with our hands.

Instructors of pottery craft will tell how it is essential to let learners have a period of 'play'. Kneading, thumping, stroking and polishing clay — all these are delicious, tactile experiences which adults have long abandoned and which they can now rediscover without inhibitions in a classroom setting.

INSTRUCTING IN SKILL WHEN TOUCH IS IMPORTANT

But there is another, more intriguing feature which distinguishes touch from all other senses. Because of the private, essentially exclusive nature of touch, because of the direct physical connection of the body of the toucher with the object touched, it follows that only one person can touch and experience one particular object at a time. Any number of people may gaze at an object, and any number of people listen at once to a sound. But it is you, and you alone who are sensing, feeling this book as you handle it. You feel it in a unique way that no-one else can.

This fact has important implications for instructors teaching skills relying on touch. The instructor must allow the earliest possible opportunity for genuine experience on the part of the learner. The learner has to feel, to touch, and to handle for himself. He has to experience directly for himself. No abstract words or long-winded explanations are of any use here. Direct experience is the order of the day. Good instructors never hesitate to let the touch experience speak for itself to the learner, directly.

SKILL INSTRUCTION: AN EXAMPLE OF USING TOUCH

I once overheard a motor body repair instructor showing a mature trainee how to use the sense of touch to detect unevenness in a repaired dent in a car wing which the trainee had extensively filled with cellulose filler. To the eye the dull matt finish of the filler and the surrounding matted-off paintwork visibly revealed neither surface unevenness nor incorrect contours.

Yet in the judgement of the instructor the job was far from satisfactory. He explained that when the high gloss finishing paint was finally sprayed on all unevenness would appear magnified. There was only one sure way to find faults at this stage and that was by feel. At this point the instructor decided to start the trainee developing the acute sense of touch that all really first-class car body repairers need.

'Try it,' said the instructor. 'Run your hand over it.' Acting on this the trainee rapidly felt the patch in question then withdrew his hand quickly.

'Feels fine to me,' he said gingerly.

The instructor paused for effect. He then said quietly and firmly, 'Look, this is something you've made. You've created it. It's yours. It isn't a piece of sculpture in a museum that you're not supposed to touch or feel. Nobody is going to shout at you. You've made it, you enjoy it. Feel it, let it communicate to you — here, like this . . .'

The instructor then slowly ran the flat part of his fingertips, then his whole hand, along the surface. He started at a point long before the repaired area and ended long after. He repeated the process two, three times, each time savouring the flow of the contours, the minute unevenness in the surface. As he was doing this he was explaining that he was letting himself become more than normally aware of the sense of touch. As he so effectively put it, he was 'reading' with his fingertips and palms.

Suddenly he stopped and turned to the trainee, smiling. 'Yes, there is an uneven patch there. But you don't need me to point it out to you, do you? You will be able to feel it for yourself this time. Take your time — and have fun!'

TIPS FOR INSTRUCTION

☐ The sense-experience of touch speaks for itself: always give it a chance!

☐ Many skills relying on touch need the correct hand pressure to be applied (for example in body-massage or throwing clay on a potter's wheel). Often the most effective way to instruct is to take the hands of the learner and guide them.

Stage 2: the central role of the brain

When we examine closely how to undertake skills a striking feature emerges. We find that often we do not rely on one sense alone during the course of the skill. Instead we will switch from one sense to another!

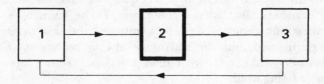

For example in bread making there comes a time when just looking at the crust of a loaf will not tell us if it is baked to perfection. A light tap with the knuckles will tell us more about the inside of the loaf. Here we have switched from the sense of vision to the sense of hearing.

This process of 'switching' senses is important in being able to perform thousands of common skills successfully.

Telling the learner about switching senses

Frequently when inexperienced or untrained persons are instructing they will omit to tell the learner clearly and unambiguously which sense they should be attending to.

It is easy to forget to do this when instructing someone. This is simply because the instructor is skilled in the activity or task in question and can perform it unconsciously, without having to think about which senses need to be attended to.

The poor learner, though, has not reached this stage of development and often he is left floundering, not knowing what to attend to; not knowing what to 'filter out' or ignore. Skilled performers do not realize that over time and with practice of their craft or skill they have learned to attend to certain senses with highly developed precision; they focus on certain kinds of information, reject lots of other information.

You will find this error taking place in the following exchange so often overheard between an instructor and learner. The instructor knows inside out the skill being taught, has been practising it for years, but when he or she begins to explain it things begin to go wrong.

Learner: Tell me what this is for?
Instructor: I don't worry about that.
Learner: And this?
Instructor: No, forget about that. That comes later.
Learner: But what about this, here?
Instructor: Not just yet, you don't need it.

It is the typical question and answer familiar to us all in many contexts. But what is happening? The learner eagerly asks questions about what is happening as the skill or task is being performed, but the instructor always replies by telling the learner what *not* to attend to; what senses are not currently being used.

What helps the learner much more is being told what directly to attend to. Don't wait for him to ask, direct his attention at the outset. This kind of direction is especially valuable in the early stages of skill instruction.

Below is an example of one instructor deliberately getting the learner to switch his attention from one sense to another. Note how carefully the instructor makes sure the learner understands or 'reads' the sensations he is referring to. Notice too how the order in which the senses are to be used is made clear to the learner.

SKILL INSTRUCTION: SWITCHING SENSES

An instructor *(I)* was demonstrating to a learner *(L)* the basic activities involved in metal turning on a centre lathe.

(I) After bringing the cutting tool up to the metal you rotate the wheel to begin to cut. When cutting starts — see the cut metal coming off in curls? — you feed the tool in slowly, evenly, using two hands. Can you see the tool advancing as I do it?
(L) Yes.

(I) You can now feel it gently cutting into the metal through your hands on the wheel, like I am doing now. You can also hear the even cutting sound ... Hear it?
(L) Yes, I can hear.
(I) So you turn on three senses on after another. You are looking at the even curl of the metal cut coming off the cutting tool. You are feeling the tool cutting through your hands on the wheel. Finally you are listening to the sound of the cut. Here, have a go yourself.

The role of the brain in skills is not wholly concerned with selecting the right sense-channel. It is also engaged in the enormously important process of planning and initiating activity.

The role of the brain in planning skills

We are most familiar with the mental activity of planning in the context of, for instance, planning a meal or planning a holiday. Here we are engaged in trying to anticipate requirements, or in trying to foresee unexpected events. In short, planning is mentally preparing ourselves for the future.

It is exactly the same with skills, for in the same way there is a forward-looking planning component to even our most humble everyday skills. The more accomplished and skilled we become at a task then the more our actions are organized with reference to the immediate future; the more plans and forethought count. Let us examine any skill we undertake with our hands done in a fairly rapid manner. Bricklaying, weaving, plastering or painting will supply the examples. What happens as the skill is performed?

☐ Skilled performers will use anticipatory vision. They will quickly scan the part of the job still to be done, before they even start it. This allows them to plan and organize how they are going to tackle it before they do it. Mentally they are one step ahead.
☐ By planning ahead they can think out their moves. They need only make those movements which are absolutely necessary.
☐ The thoughts of the performers are directed more towards the future; they give fewer backward glances to see if what they have just done is right.

Contrast this with the performance of an absolute beginner. How does he tackle the skill?

☐ Jerky, often seemingly random movements.
☐ Hesitation and cautious progress throughout the task.
☐ Many backward glances to see if everything is completed correctly.

The knowledge that there are distinct phases to acquiring a skill such as outlined above, can be of help to you the instructor. For once novices have passed the fumbling stage of an absolute beginner, they can gently be introduced to thinking more about their future actions, to planning more as they perform the skill. Chapter 6 looks at techniques for doing this.

Rhythms in skills

We must note also that with advancing experience in a skill the brain often seeks to organize activity into a rhythm. For the really skilled performer the rhythms of the task are its inbuilt metronome. Consider some examples we find around us performed every day.

☐ A bricklayer will pause after laying a brick immediately before scooping up fresh cement on the trowel.
☐ A painter will pause momentarily after loading a brush with paint.
☐ Scraping potatoes in a bowl of water — the quick dips into the water to wash the scrapings off punctuate the task.

All these are occasions for a slight pause in the natural cycle of activity. It is these pauses which help to give skills the fluid, graceful rhythms which we find so pleasurable to watch.

H Belloc, writing in 1906, notes this accurately:

'Mowing is a thing of ample gestures, like drawing a cartoon.
Then, again, get yourself into a mechanical and repetitive mood:
be thinking of anything at all but your mowing, and be anxious
only when there seems some interruption to the monotony of the
sound.'

(H Belloc *The mowing of a field*, 1906)

The instructor can be of great help to the learner if he can draw his attention to the rhythms or cycles of activity which are contained in many skills.

Stage 3: the output stage

The actions and muscular activities performed in skills ought to be described first, because whenever we look at a person performing a skill it is the public activity, the output, which we see and notice first of all.

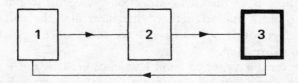

It can be said that in industry there is a decline in the use of skills which need brute physical strength for output. This is due mostly to mechanization and automation. The skills increasingly at a premium in industry are the skills of controlling machines, monitoring controls and making logical decisions.

But is there a corresponding change in the output of skills used in everyday life? Clearly we can see that even in home-based skills, mechanization has taken place.

Home-based skills

We can classify home-based skills into three broad types. First, we have simple unaided handwork skills. There the output is physical unaided action by the performer. Modelling clay by hand or knotting are examples. Next come handwork skills which use hand tools (including musical instruments). Finally there are those skills relying on handwork supplemented by electric power tools. Let us examine the kinds of output required by the last two.

HANDWORK WITH HAND TOOLS

Tools can be relatively low in mechanical sophistication, for example a hammer or pair of garden shears. They can be higher in mechanical sophistication. Examples here would be hydraulic jacks, hand lawn-mowers or pumps. What does the use of these tools tell us about the nature of the output of the human operators?

Broadly speaking the gross physical activity remains the same. We have to propel chisels, aim hammers with accuracy, just as we have to work pumps and jacks or propel hand

49

lawn-mowers. What is important for instruction is that with the more sophisticated mechanical tools, a knowledge of the principles of their working actually aids the learner to acquire the skill. Now the mechanical principles of the more sophisticated tools are not as readily apparent as those of simple tools.

For instance, to anyone learning to hammer a nail into wood there is an obvious connection between the aim of the hammer blow, the strength of the blow and the end result. This connection is not so easy to see when more sophisticated hand tools are used.

Take certain types of hand lawn-mower. It is not a matter of brute physical strength to cut a tall patch of grass. Rather it requires a knowledge of momentum – a knowledge that the mechanism (hidden sometimes) incorporates a flywheel to smooth out momentum. The action required is not a brute shoving forward from a standstill, but rather a backward then forward movement using and maintaining momentum.

HANDWORK WITH ELECTRIC TOOLS

The increasing home ownership of power tools has had a revolutionary effect on our everyday skills. It is comparable in many ways to the effect of industrialization on manufacturing skills in the 18th century.

Our actions and output in using the wide range of home power tools are slowly changing. Because industrialization and technology now intrude into our homes we are increasingly called upon to demonstrate monitoring skills, control skills or decision skills.

A change in output

The amount of human output or action required to operate our electric gadgetry or electric tools differs considerably. At one extreme the electric tools require a fairly large amount of human effort or action. A power drill is an obvious example. We have to supply the positioning force and the thrust; the electric motor supplies the rotation of the drill bit.

At the other extreme there are common electric tools which require only the minimum of physical input – but correspondingly more planning skills. Physically loading an automatic washing machine, then deciding on and selecting the appropriate programme is one example. At the 'fully automatic' extreme the proportion of action required by the operator becomes even less. For example, a fully automatic camera estimates exposure required and computes and selects the correct aperture – we only have to supply the pressure on the shutter trigger. Our output is minimal, the rest is done for us.

The future

The kinds of skills and outputs we will need in the future will change. Increasingly we will be instructing in skills which use sophisticated machinery and electronic gadgetry. Motor-driven tools will become more common. So too will the video-camera, the home video-recorder, the portable computer. The microprocessor and home computer in turn, will revolution-ize our home access to information and stored knowledge. Developments in technology in these fields will inevitably bring more of the world into our homes.

With this will come a change in the kinds of activities and skills needed on our part. Skills and activities will become mental. Increasingly our outputs as humans will be the com-prehension of instruments, the monitoring and understanding of visual displays, the manipulation of controls.

The activities here put the emphasis squarely on higher, more mental kinds of learning. New exciting kinds of learning and instruction will be needed. These are explained in Chapter 5.

Stage 4: feedback

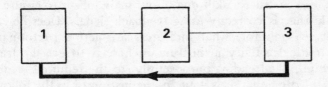

Perhaps the most important element in our model is the link between the output of our actions and telling whether they are right or wrong. For instance, all the while we are painting, hammering, driving or carving we are monitoring and watching closely how well we are doing. While doing this, of course, we are continually changing what we are doing. We alter the angle

51

of hammer blows, we vary the force applied, we alter the angle of cut of the chisel as we carve, and so on. In short, we are monitoring our output and varying what we do (the input) according to what is required.

Feedback information

The real issue for instructors is to make sure that the learner knows what signals, what information he is to attend to. Let us illustrate this by the common example of driving a car.

Suppose you are driving along a straight road. Slight variations in camber, road surface and wind will inevitably cause the car to wander off the intended course. Our visual sense (the input) signals that we are deviating from the desired course. A rapid estimation on our part of the amount of deviation is followed by a corrective turn of the wheel (undertaken by the motor activity of steering). As we head back on course we might sense either under- or over-correction in our response. The process is therefore repeated.

Driving is a skill which involves the intricate use of feedback — feedback of our actions that is not just through the visual sense alone. We monitor continually, and are ready to act on, information relayed through our ears ('is the engine revving too high?'), the contact of our bodies with the car seat ('am I cornering too fast?'). All these signals are taken note of in the brain. They are analysed, processed, and we act by performing the correct remedial action on the car controls.

Learners using feedback

When we instruct a skill one of our main jobs is to ensure that the learner is correctly using feedback signals. Does he know what to look for, what indicates satisfactory performance? The critical activity in instruction here is to get the learner 'cued in', or attending purposefully, to the required feedback signal. Note how this is done by the instructor in the following example.

SKILL INSTRUCTION: ATTENDING TO THE CORRECT FEEDBACK

A driving instructor was instructing an absolute beginner. He noticed that whenever the learner selected neutral he looked down to the position of the gear lever. On occasions he even looked at the gear position diagram printed on the dashboard in order to locate the gears.

This distracting habit was hindering learning and would certainly prove a positive danger when the vehicle was moving. The instructor needed to get the learner attending to the right feedback signals. This is what he was overheard to say:

'What you have to do is get the gear-box inside your own body. You need to know where the gears are without looking down. The position of your arm and the slight resistance as you engage gear tell you all you need to know. There is no need to look. Shut your eyes and change up and down. Get the gear-box fixed in your body. Go on, try it. Tell me out loud what you are doing. Do you feel the slight resistance before you enter the gear? Can you find the slack feeling of neutral?'

Instructors should note the following points about feedback:

☐ Does the learner know what to look for, is he able to discriminate a right from a wrong performance?
☐ It sometimes helps if the learner can talk about how he is understanding the feedback signals. Like our example, this will show if he is understanding feedback correctly, recognizing the connection between what he has done and the results.

Conclusion

An instructor should look analytically at the skill or activity he is demonstrating. He should look for four parts. Firstly, he should examine the kinds of senses being used, the input of information used in the skill.

Next he must ask about the role of the brain in skills. Does the learner have to switch consciously between the kinds of senses used as he performs the skill? Is there any planning or thinking ahead or are there any rhythms that the brain can use to organize the skill effectively?

Thirdly, the instructor must examine the kinds of output required by the skill. Is there any particular type needed? Is there special learning needed?

Lastly, the instructor must look at feedback information. What information or results tell the learner if he is right or wrong? Does the learner know how to use this information, can he 'read' it and learn from his mistakes?

Every instructor should look methodically, analytically, at whatever skill or activity he is instructing. When the skill is split up into its four component parts it becomes much easier to understand and explain.

Successful instruction is not far away.

References

Belloc, H (1906) *The Pyrenees*. Faber. London.

Stammers, R and Patrick, J (1975) *The Psychology of Training*. Methuen, London.

Welford, A T (1968) *Fundamentals of Skill*. Methuen, London.

Further Reading

Belbin, R M and Belbin, E (1968) *Problems in Adult Retraining*. Heinemann, London.

Drowatsky, J N (1975) *Motor Learning: Principles and Practises*. Burgess, Minneapolis.

Holding, D H (1965) *Principles of Training*. Pergamon Press, Oxford.

Miller, R B (1962) Task Descriptions and Analysis. In Gagné, R M (ed) *Psychological Principles in System Development*. Rinehart & Winston, New York.

Seymour, W J (1966) *Industrial Skills*. Pitman, London.

Wellens, J (1974) *Training in Physical Skills*. Business Books, London.

Chapter 4

Getting started

Overview: Before we analyse our skill and commence instruction
it is useful if we ask ourselves a few basic questions about how
we are going to proceed: Am I fully prepared for the task ahead?
How am I going to let the learners know they are progressing
correctly? How am I going to let them know they are wrong? Is
there anything I can do beforehand to make my instruction more
effective? Can I encourage the learners to help each other?

Introduction

To start the chapter off I want to confront you with a direct
question. What was, in your experience, the best piece of
detailed, practical instruction you have ever received in your
life? I am asking not for the instruction that had the most far-
reaching consequences, but instead that piece of instruction
which you personally hold as a superlative example of the art.

This may sound a little bold, but there is one feature that
will be common to every example recalled. The one common
feature is thorough and exhaustive preparation on the part of
the instructor. It is the one thing that makes the instruction
endure in the minds of you, the learners. Thorough preparation may be concealed (as so much painstaking preparation
is), but its effects are lasting and permanent. Inadequately
prepared and poorly delivered instruction is, and always will
be, an unmitigating disaster. True, we can all recall such
disasters — the perplexed instructor, the bemused teacher, the
collapsing model, the malfunctioning projector, the snapping
tool or appliance. All of these are instructional catastrophes.
We remember the disasters, the embarrassment, the 'faux pas' —
but we never remember the content of instruction. What
sticks in our minds forever is always cool, clear, methodical
easy-to-remember instruction.

This is the desired role model. But the goal does not come
easily. Good clear instruction; a smoothly executed essentially polished performance rarely, if ever, comes naturally.
Like any performance it has to be worked upon, prepared for.
So let us start with the obvious. So obvious in fact that it is
easily overlooked: is everything you are going to need in good

condition and ready to hand? We can summarize these needs as time, tools and technology.

Time, tools and technology

Before you apportion time for instruction in a skill or part of a skill remember that novice instructors consistently under-estimate how long learners need. Instructors constantly say that they have only achieved a mere fraction of what they set out to. Now it is not necessarily the half-completed instruc-tional goal that is such a bad thing, instead it is the frustration and personal anxiety felt on the part of the instructor which is damaging. The word damaging is used because instructor frustration communicates itself to the learner. It is the learner who bears the ultimate brunt of this frustration; it is the learner who feels inadequate, begins to get a mysterious feeling of under achievement. The instructor for his part may not deliberately set out to communicate that he has only achieved the merest fraction, but the message gets through somehow.

Always be generous with time. Today time is a precious commodity and many of your learners will be from environ-ments fraught with hassle and time pressure. Give them a precious luxury so few of us can afford — a generous time-space in which to look, to listen, ask questions, make mistakes, laugh and correct them. Give them time to reflect on per-formance, to stop and study a skilled performance. Practically it means that you should: always allow a margin of time for interruptions (there will be); allow time for late arrivals and slowcoaches (there will be); allow time for requests for reruns (there will be); allow time for the smart, difficult questions which take you ages to answer (there will be).

Deciding how long to allow for an instructional session is difficult. Usually novice instructors report that their initial estimations had been out by as much as a half. They esti-mated an hour but needed in practice at least an hour and a half. Only careful, generous apportionment of time will allow you to engineer a calm, unhurried atmosphere.

Tools and equipment needed for your instructional session will almost certainly be dictated by the nature of the skill being taught, but it is always good practice to get into the habit of checking everything over before you commence. Are all the tools to hand, are they sharp and in perfect condition?

Remember that it is you who are the skilled performer and as such you may well be able to handle less-than-perfect tools and implements. It is easy to overlook the fact that over the years you have learned to accommodate blunt, inaccurate, tired and shabby tools. To you alone they have a familiar feel. To the newcomer such trivial-seeming impediments will be magnified into insurmountable hurdles.

The selection and use of appropriate training technology — whether it be video, slides or film is beyond the scope of this book and has been adequately reviewed elsewhere (Romiszowski 1987). In using training technology 'Sod's law' will always apply: if there is anything at all to go wrong with the mechanism then it will go wrong. The rule here seems again to thoroughly check everything over before the session — never immediately on entering the training room, studio or workshop. This is a habit that should be with you throughout your instructional career.

Instructional goals

At this point it is useful to pause and to review what your goals in instruction are. Overall goal setting in instruction will be determined largely by organizational constraints. 'I am only allowed three weekly sessions of two hours each to get my syllabus/skill across'. What concerns us here is the question of goal setting for each session. As we shall see in the following chapter most skills can be broken down into sub-goals using the process called task analysis. It is useful to ask at the outset, however, if there are any natural sub-goals or milestones in the acquisition of the skill. But why should we actively seek these out? What, if any, are the advantages of seeking out milestones in instruction? It is simply because it is a real human need in any task — be it work or play — to break tasks down into manageable units. If the skill yields definite sub-goals use them as simple targets for your learners to aim for. Let them serve as points of attainment, vantage points, from which to take stock of what they have gained. It is easy to overlook the value of these to the novice and it cannot be over stressed to the beginning instructor. Here are some common sub-goals selected by instructors:

Bricklaying: laying three or four bricks 'to the line' level.

Swimming: perfecting first leg movements, then arm movements separately.
Time trial cycling: holding the optimum cadence of 80 revolutions per minute for one kilometre.

However, beware, segmenting skills in this way is not without its dangers. Too small segments, too easily reached goals will have the effect of demotivating the learner. The easy reaching of too numerous sub-goals leads to what we call the 'pall effect'. If the goal is too easy, the challenge is drawn. Conversely, set too large and distant a sub-goal and the learner will be overwhelmed and demoralized. The real skill of instruction comes in grading the challenge to the learner's capacity: juggling with the reachable goals yet stretching the learner. Chapter 7 examines among other things how best to space the sub-goals for each type of learner.

At this stage many readers will be daunted by the size of the job ahead. Sub-goals, task analysis, matching instruction to learner needs — the list of do's and don'ts seem endless and intimidating. There is no need to be daunted though. Have confidence in your own abilities, you will quickly realize the tremendously wide range of learning capacities people have and part of the fun and reward of becoming a first-rate instructor lies in gaining a widening repertoire of instructional techniques.

Pre-instructional strategies

In all instruction in practical skills, whether it be vocational or recreational, there is usually a distinct episode which takes place before instruction actually commences. (Here it is assumed that proper social contact has been made as outlined in Chapter 2). This episode can take many forms: it can consist of a short introductory talk, it may take the form of a demonstration of the whole skill, it might be a mini-lecture on the main key points, or be a talk on health and safety aspects, it might take the form of a 'reading of the riot act' (threats and warnings) or a lecture on hazards and dangers. All of these myriad events take place essentially before serious face-to-face instruction begins. All of these widely differing introductory episodes have a common name: pre-instructional srategies. This rather daunting title belies the immense utility they have for the instructor.

First they serve to introduce you in a proper, professional capacity. Unlike the social chat, the contact-making session over coffee or tea or enrolment, here is where you begin business.

Second, because of the above, you should gain the attention of the learner in a way essentially different from that before. Focused attention with distractions removed should characterize this pre-instructional episode.

Third, the pre-instructional session is a great leveller. If you are instructing a group, they are brought together for the first time to start from the same point. To take a horse-racing analogy, the group are assembled for the first time 'under starter's orders'.

The fourth and final use is that here are your learners assembled collectively for the first time ready to have their attention directed in the way that you and nobody else wants. You have both the power and the responsibility that follows from this. Expectation is therefore unbelievably high in these sessions.

Overviews

The first pre-instructional strategy we shall examine are those that we call 'overviews'. Overviews are just what they mean: they exist to let the learner see overall the whole skill or learning goal in advance. It allows a little perspective or distance in on the skill. As the name suggests it lets the learner see the whole, lets them see how things fit together and should look when complete. No attempt is made to dismember the skill or analyse it. The goal is to let the learner see the whole event, as it is executed, in as near-perfect a way as is possible.

An overview is best used when you are confident that the learner can appreciate it for what it is. To have the whole skill or learning goal performed by an expert (you) can be daunting and off putting. It can lead to groans of the 'Oh I shall never able to do all that' sort. Used judiciously though, overviews can work wonders. The instructor in Origami we encountered earlier, was using an overview to wonderful effect. He used it to have both an alerting and a challenging effect simultaneously. 'Here before you is all that I am going to show you. Watch.' He quickly, deftly, folded paper methodically first once, then twice. He then chatted amiably through the exercise, performing neat, tricky pulls and pushes of the paper until two tantalizing tabs of paper were left, just waiting to be pulled. These he pulled with all the histrionic aplomb of the magician. The final paper form appeared, to gasps of delight from the audience, even a ripple of applause. 'Right, now let's take it step by step. Ready?'

If the introductory overview lets the learner have a 'bird's eye view' of the whole, then there is another pre-instructional technique which aims to abstract the principles or the bare bones of the skill. These are when the instructor precedes his instruction with words such as 'Now the key to understanding all there is to know about . . .'. Often life or death safety aspects are introduced in this way. One instructor commenced instruction in using a chain saw by saying 'Safety aspects are crucial. Always stand firm, balanced on both feet, spread slightly.'

An example

Such an attempt at 'laying bare' crucial elements of the skill is called an 'advance organizer' and can be found at work in the following ways: an instructor in techniques of slalom canoeing was demonstrating rolling techniques. 'There is one key thing to remember when you are upside down, underwater in the boat — DO NOT PANIC! It is perfectly safe, you cannot drown. You cannot become wedged in the boat, you will float out naturally. You can get yourself out with the minimum of difficulty and discomfort AND come up smiling if you follow this simple three point routine. One, Two, Three. Here we go . . .!'

The overall role

Pre-instructional strategies have an important part to play in the overall instructional goal. Short and brief though they may be they remain a key attention-getting device. Always remember though that it might well be the first close-up contact the learner has with the skill. Pre-instructional strategies (like for example the brief description of a film on television printed in the newspaper which can surely be construed as an overview) can have far reaching effects. Strategies can and do shake our preconceptions to the foundations; strategies can and do challenge us, and they can even structure the whole way we approach what is to follow. Many polished instructors play up to this. However you will quickly learn after experimenting, what particular strategy suits you, your skill and your learners.

Learners as resources

You, the reader are an acknowledged expert at your skill. You have been selected to be the ambassador of the skill in question. Many instructors need gentle reminding that they exist to give the skill away: the instructor's loss is the learner's gain. Once an instructor acknowledges this he is abandoning the idea of the skill as being his own exclusive property. Instructors who are ready to acknowledge this also acknowledge that there are learners around who might quickly turn out to be as perfect executors of the skill as they are. Indeed they might even become better! To realize this point is only one step away from realizing the greatest asset in skill instruction is not instructors themselves — but the learners. If the right atmosphere — non-competitive, co-operative, mutually supportive — is nurtured in groups of learners, then people positively delight in showing one another what they have learnt. Once something has fallen into place, once mastery has been achieved, then it is a natural response for people to want to communicate it to others. Indeed, given the right atmosphere it is almost impossible to stop it happening. 'I've just realized I've been attempting to do it wrong all along. That is why I have been struggling so. It is like this, here let me show you.' It is this sort of response among groups of learners that betrays this feeling.

The learners, once they have correctly mastered the skill or task in hand, then become the most powerful allies the instructor can ever have. Despite the instructors' well-meaning attempts at making social contact, despite their wishes to surmount barriers — instructors are, and always will be, different from learners. There is a certain insurmountable barrier of authority and status. The instructor has status, the instructor is paid, and in a thousand and one other ways differences exist. But sitting next to the learner is another learner, just like himself. A learner, who like him, is probably frustrated, who is tired and likewise struggling with the skill. The odd word of encouragement, the odd explanation from someone who is on an equal footing, is worth its weight in gold.

People's readiness to learn from their peers should always be acknowledged and welcomed. Do not see it as a threat to usurping your position as instructor. It should not be construed as an attempt to upstage you, to steal the show, to put you out of a job. Look on it instead as a resource to be used creatively, for when peer learning is unleashed in a group, dramatic results can be witnessed, as the following example illustrates.

An example

One instructor was giving a course on business microcomputer skills — word processing, spreadsheets, simple database manipulation. The special instructional requirements for so-called high technology skills have been described in detail elsewhere (Winfield 1986). The layout of the microcomputer workshop was unusual in that the workshop had once been two separate rooms, and now had a single door knocked through. The two halves had about 10 microcomputers in each, and it happened by chance that the class had distributed itself in roughly the same composition of age, sex and experience across the two halves. The instructor decided he had a ready-made environment to undertake a simple learning experiment.

The instructor's normal routine with the practical skill of teaching microcomputer applications packages was to leave the learners to battle on individually in relative isolation. One half of the workshop he left to their own devices: giving assistance where necessary, sorting out wrangles, pointing out how to use the self-instruction materials and user-manuals. The room was quiet and studious. Progress however was painful and slow.

He entered the other half of the workshop and closed the adjoining door behind him. 'Can I have your attention for a moment? Let me explain how these workshops are designed. We call them workshops because the emphasis is on all of us learning together, helping each other out and trying to co-operate. If you find something out, help your neighbour who may be struggling with the same thing. I can only deal with one person at a time and I shall be making my progress round the room as quickly as possible, but don't be afraid to ask each other for help. Remember that there is no competition to finish first. If you find yourself getting ahead turn and help the slower ones. You all know the saying "You don't know something until you have had to explain it to someone else".

Well, it can be a good way of fixing what you have learned yourself. Have a go.'

As the course progressed over the weeks the contrast between the two halves could not have been more marked. The first half laboured on in studious silence. A silence punctuated only by the regular tap, tap, tap of the computer keyboard and the occasional gasp of frustration. On the whole it was silent, sweated labour. Overall progress in this half was slow.

However, the second half behaved — in the words of the instructor 'as if a genie had been unleashed'. People were milling round, peering at screens, leaning across to their neighbour comparing findings. Requests were vocalized, advice shouted out, 'I'm finding a quick way to get back into the main menu. Just tap 'return' twice, quickly'. The atmosphere was alive with discussion and sharing.

This example is by no means the definitive answer on the issue of peer learning. In many ways the 'learning experiment' was poorly controlled and our second group in the peer learning half were engaged in the process we called discovery learning. (This is explained more fully in Chapter 7.) As a group they were largely ignoring the text-based instruction and instead 'finding out for themselves'. It might have been this, rather than the peer learning atmosphere, that contributed to their relative success. The experiment had a salutary effect on our instructor. Thereafter he vowed to view learners as potent resources to be harnessed, and he vowed to use them whenever conditions permitted. He became a better instructor for it, too.

Conclusion

The process of harnessing confederates in helping you instruct is not without its dangers. The readiness with which learners learn from peers is fraught with dangers — some obvious, some hidden. The biggest danger, of course, is of the learners being instructed incorrectly by their well-meaning, enthusiastic peers. Learners who master the skill or segment of the skill are of course only too pleased to demonstrate their new found prowess to others and to help ailing colleagues. Make doubly sure if you are using confederates that they are demonstrating perfect mastery of the skill before unleashing them on the rest. While your back is turned one over-enthusiastic helper can quickly instruct the whole class, but in the wrong method!

Carefully check that they instruct correctly before you launch them off on their own endeavours. Remember that it is in the early, crucial stages of skill learning that wrong procedures, once learnt, are difficult to unlearn. It is a burden on both learner and instructor to have to go round and correct incorrectly learnt methods.

Knowledge of results

Considering the important issues of close guidance and explanations brings us to examine, in more depth, the concept of knowledge of results first introduced in the previous chapter. One of the reasons the peer learning group in the illustration of microcomputer skills did so well is that they had immediate knowledge of whether they were right or wrong. They did not have to progress far in learning the skill before feedback was given. The group left to their manuals and intermittent visits by the instructor, floundered in isolation. Feedback was very infrequent.

A generally high level of vocalization in our peer learning group ensured rapid and close feedback of results: the high level of social interaction ensured learners were immediately in contact with their progress. Deprive any learner of knowledge of their progress and despair quickly follows – this has been demonstrated in countless studies of how people learn. The instructor's job is always to find out if the learner is using feedback effectively. Does the learner know immediately if they are right or wrong? Do they know how to interpret the signals and cues which tell them if they are correct or not? Is the learner finding out for himself the feel or look for the machine or tool and if it is functioning correctly? So often in early instruction you hear the instructor asking questions like: 'Now, can you feel it respond correctly?' 'When you hold your body correctly, you can feel it working properly. That is the thing to aim for.'

Let us examine the major types of knowledge of results. To return to our computer workshop example once more, we see that this demonstrated two kinds. Learners in one half of the workshop received intermittent knowledge of results only. Knowledge of results was saved up by the instructor to be given in intermittent 'doses' as he encountered each learner on his rounds. 'You are doing fine, you have come a long way since I saw you last.' Or, more likely we hear him utter phrases like 'Oh dear, we have gotten ourselves in quite a tangle since the last time haven't we?'

The peer group experienced knowledge of results that was characterized by its vocalized immediacy. 'Oops I've lost the main menu again — what was the quick way of getting it back?' Back came the laconic reply from the learner at the neighbouring microcomputer: 'Just press escape and it will come up again eventually...'.

Now some skills let the learner know admirably well how they are doing as they are doing it — feedback and knowledge of results is both immediate and visible. For instance as you are learning to use the woodworking plane the even, regular curls of planed wood issuing from the plane give instant guidance on a smooth, even stroke and action. Any task involving steering or tracking is the same. Contrast this with, say, the ballistic skill of shooting a gun or hitting a ball with a racket or bat. Here the feedback or knowledge of right or wrong aiming technique or batting technique comes not quite immediately. Instead it is slightly delayed — essentially it comes a few seconds or fraction of a second in the resultant trajectory of bullet, arrow, ball, shuttlecock etc. Feedback, and hence knowledge of results, is delayed. It is however intimately connected to the execution of the task. It is up to the instructor to explain and point out the connection.

If we listen carefully to the full meaning behind instructors' comments we can witness this process in action. Imagine that our trainee has fired a gun at a practice target. Immediately afterwards the instructor comments, 'Do you realize that you wandered off target as you actually squeezed the trigger? You loosened your grip on the barrel and sights were lowered. Can you see how it happened? Hold tight with one hand and squeeze with the other.'

Here we hear the instructor undertaking the archetypal instructor role: alerting learner perceptions to the connection between the execution of the action and the actual (delayed) knowledge of results. The rule for instructors appears to be — always be on the look out for intrinsic knowledge of results that appear as the task is being undertaken. Endeavour to point these out, vocalize and carefully describe these as they appear.

Other ways of giving feedback

In giving knowledge of results instructors have to make a fundamental choice. It is a choice often made unconsciously, but it is a choice nevertheless. It is between whether to give feedback on performance verbally or non-verbally. We often find that novice instructors usually opt for the former. It is as if their image of the instructor is one of talker, vocalizer, explainer. Here their incorrect stereotype leads them to make a very basic error in choice of mode of feedback: they fall into the trap of over-reliance on verbal feedback alone.

What do they do? Despite their well-meaning intentions they simply overdo things. They subject the poor struggling learner to a veritable torrent of advice — continually talking right through the learning process. Needless to say this can be extremely off-putting to the learner who often will not complain because of status incongruity and plain shyness. This type of instructor behaviour — over-talking, over-explaining — debases the currency of the words of the instructor. Learners have strictly limited capacity to attend to information; they, more than anyone else are operating at the very limits of concentration and attention. I once followed an instructor round a small class learning joinery skills. The instructor was engaged in a continual torrent of advice. Scrupulously close guidance was being given, irrespective of their needs, to everyone in the class. He was driven by the desire to give as much verbal advice as was possible — the result was nothing short of the learners being swamped with information. The result on the part of the instructor must have been hoarseness and a sore throat. Although his intentions were noble it must have given the class earache. 'Oops. Watch it there, you are over the line.' Quickly he moved on to the next learner. 'Yes, yes, that's better. Up a bit, down. Hold it.' Then the next person. 'Hold it tighter, tighter, that's better. Oops, you let it slip.' On and on it went, an incessant chatter as busy as a skylark's warble. But much more wearing on the nerves.

Of course all novice instructors are keenly aware of the role of verbal explanations. They see it as an integral part of their vocation, and rightly so. But the key to effective instruction is the judicious use of language. Language is, and always will be, the most effective vehicle of communication between humans. But it is not the only channel of communication available, and novice instructors are well advised to periodically

review other means. To switch the means of giving information, encouragement and feedback to learners can have a
surprisingly alerting effect. If the eyes of the learner are
riveted on the tool, the machine or suchlike, then giving
knowledge of results by talking to them in a non-distracting
manner seems sensible. The learner does not have to take his
eyes off the critical object or feature in order to get knowledge
of results. But always be aware of the occasions where this
may not be case. There may be times when other channels of
communication can be better employed. Sometimes a smile,
a nod, a pat on the back, the 'thumbs up' sign says it all —
and more eloquently, too. The point to note here is to be
aware that we can vary the method of giving feedback; novelty
and unpredictability keeps people on their toes. Giving feedback in the same, tired manner quickly loses its reinforcing
effect. The instructor in the previous example relying wholly
on the verbal mode, quickly ran out of superlatives when
commending his learners. For their part his praise rapidly lost
its value. 'That's great. That's fine. That's excellent. That's
wonderful. That's ace.' His repertoire was quickly exhausted;
his learners were quickly bored.

There is no standard theory to guide us in when, how, and
if, to use non-verbal feedback. The answer lies in your own
observations — of how other effective instructors operate.
There is no better, more effective way of increasing the repertoire of instructional skills than by observing others, trying
their techniques and discarding, adapting and modifying what
you see.

The highly skilled first-rate instructor, by using this process
of observation, trial and error, is alive to a whole range of ways
of communicating; often using non-verbal ways that to the
casual observer would go unnoticed. To many people how
they achieve what they do is something of a mystery. But to
you, embarking on a career in instruction, it should be a
continual source of fascination.

An example

This last example is from sport. It concerns the briefest of
behaviour by a football team manager/coach. The setting and
the context of this particular example of use of non-verbal
feedback might seem a far cry from mundane day-to-day
instruction, but the lesson is there for us all to learn.

The manager's team had won through to the cup final at Wembley, UK. The team were the 'underdogs' from a smallish town facing a team from a large city which had won the cup the previous year. A full season of hard training and careful instruction and coaching had preceded the match. At the end of the match the two teams had drawn; both teams had played themselves to exhaustion. Before extra time was given to decide the winning team, a couple of minutes' rest was allowed. Team support staff ran out onto the pitch with water and team physiotherapists appeared to offer support. The two teams flopped onto the grass in utter exhaustion during which the crowd of over 60,000 supporters were uncannily quiet. There was the briefest of respites from the high drama of the game.

The manager sauntered onto the pitch, hands in pockets and wandered over to his team. What encouragement or feedback was there to give now? He had probably shouted himself hoarse throughout the game anyway. In the brief lull before the storm, words somehow seemed inadequate. One player, the key striker, lay comatose, outstretched on the grass, motionless, eyes shut. He had played until he dropped. The manager knelt down beside him and laid his hand gently on his chest, as you would to calm an infant. For a few moments the two remained still and silent.

This is an obvious example of where the manager or instructor had gauged the situation and acted accordingly, giving necessary support in an effective manner.

Praise-giving in instruction is further elaborated on in Chapter 6.

References

Romiszowski, A J (1987) *Selection and Use of Instructional Media*. 2nd Edition, Kogan Page, London.

Winfield, I J (1986) *Human Resources and Computing*. Heinemann, London.

Chapter 5
Preparing to instruct – task analysis

> **Overview:** Good instruction depends on adequate preparation. Preparation consists in examining closely the subject-matter of instruction. This chapter examines two ways of doing this, and is illustrated by some examples from everyday instruction. The process is called 'task analysis' and is the next stage in successful instruction.

Introduction

We all find ourselves at some time or other instructing other people in skills. We do it either while we are at work earning our living, or when we are at home relaxing. This chapter mainly uses examples drawn from the second of these areas — instruction that we give in and around the home, while we are entertaining or having fun with our hobbies or sports. These examples have been chosen for a special reason: we all have had experience with this type of instruction. Who, for instance, has not recently shown another person any one of the following skills? — cooking, decorating, fiddling with cars/car engines, woodwork, home plumbing, domestic appliance repair?

This kind of instruction, as we all know, is about solidly practical everyday jobs and skills. The principles governing how to instruct effectively in these skills apply equally well to more complicated and involved skills found in industry and the world of work. The rules remain the same.

The first thing we do in instruction is some careful thinking. We stop. We think about the skill we are dealing with. We think about it in terms of the input of senses, the decisions or planning skills needed, the kinds of physical output and the kinds of feedback that the learner needs to be cued in to. While we are in this thoughtful frame of mind we ask ourselves: 'Just what is it I am asking the learner to learn?':

Analysing the task (1): different kinds of learning

To the lay person all learning is the same. As with most simple beliefs the world seems to run smoothly enough by believing it.

But this is not enough for purposes of instruction. There are different kinds of learning — so different from each other that we call them by different names. Look at the following examples of learning found almost daily in any home:

- ☐ A toddler learning to tie shoe-laces.
- ☐ Learning your friend's new telephone number.
- ☐ Learning a new card game or board game.
- ☐ Learning to cook a new meal from a recipe.
- ☐ Learning how to operate a new camera.

Anyone can see that the differences are great. Some examples are simple, others complex; some examples require the learner to think hard, others less so.

Looking at learning

It is this very breadth of learning which has for centuries challenged us to understand it. Psychology attempts to classify all these different types of learning and it does this by looking at how people actually learn these various activities.

For instance, how do children learn to tie shoe-laces? What is the best way to teach them? How do we learn lists of numbers? How do we learn complicated rules and ideas? All these questions are answered by careful research. It is a process based on study and observation of people as they learn these skills.

An example of a type of learning

Here is one type of learning each of us is familiar with. It is being able to associate a simple signal or stimulus (a bell, noise, colour, etc) with a particular response or activity. For example when we see a large red sign before us it is certain that we have feelings of danger, fear or arousal. If the large red sign is an illuminated traffic signal and we are driving, then our reaction is to slow down and stop.

Lots of other signals will have their own specific effect upon us. Sudden loud noises will cause us to jump in fright or fear; the sound of a telephone ringing will serve to alert us. It is easy to forget that each of these examples has been carefully learned. Sometime in our past we have painstakingly learned to link the particular signal with the appropriate response. Strange as it may seem there was a time when we did not know what to do when the telephone rang, when we did not know what red, bold lettering signified, or what red lights looming up on the road ahead meant....

This type of learning involves us in making some sort of link between the stimulus and the response. It is a type of learning that is fairly undemanding mentally. So primitive is it that it has sometimes been referred to as 'gut learning', though we will refer to it by the name 'signal learning' (Gagné 1977).

Signal learning — how it takes place

How do we learn to respond correctly to bells, signs, noises, alarms and suchlike?

In fact we can only learn the correct thing to do if there are a sufficient number of occasions when the stimulus has been linked or paired with the appropriate response.

AN EXAMPLE OF SIGNAL LEARNING

Let us see how this happens with a common example. Signal learning takes place when very young children are taught to avoid potentially dangerous objects such as hot stoves, fires or radiators. Here the stimulus is deliberately linked with the appropriate response. The anxious parent will take the child and show it the object to be avoided often making the appropriate response for the child to imitate. This is shown in Figure 6.

STIMULUS	*linked closely with*	RESPONSE
fire		pain
radiator		avoid

'Look (*points to fire*) .... it's hot Ooch!
(*pretend hurt*)
It hurts.'

Figure 6. *Signal learning — pairing stimulus with response*

The parent will often seek to give to the child three or four pairings of the stimulus with the response — in our case showing hot fires, cooking pans, radiators, and making the same response. What the parent is doing is making sure that the child has established the link and that it can learn to

71

generalize about the danger and the need to avoid all hot objects.

Cruel though it sounds, as any parent knows, the process of linking the stimulus with the correct response can be speeded up if the child itself experiences the appropriate response — if it touches, for a second, a hot radiator. If the child eventually begins to avoid radiators and fires, and begins to utter words like 'hot', 'burn', 'hurt', when it sees these objects, the parents are both pleased and relieved. So pleased, in fact, are they that they will praise the child in some way.

Now let us examine what has taken place in this simple learning task. We can find four distinct training techniques in our example.

HOW TO INSTRUCT FOR SIGNAL LEARNING

☐ Both the name of the stimulus and the name of the response are firmly fixed to help the learner distinguish in future.

☐ The stimulus and the response are presented together.

☐ The learner is encouraged to make the correct response.

☐ When the correct response is made, praise is given.

What have we done here?

We have broken down our example into four tips for instruction. These four points apply not just to teaching children to avoid radiators or hot fires, but to all types of signal learning in both children and adults.

The hints are the actual learning conditions necessary for bringing about all examples of signal learning.

Other types of learning

But what about more complicated, higher or mental types of learning?

Will the four hints for instruction of signal learning apply to these different kinds of learning? A moment's reflection will tell us that they are inadequate. It is obvious that we learn complex activities in different ways. We do not learn to fill in income tax returns, understand complicated rules, or solve crosswords by being taken by the hand, by being shown how to respond, and by being praised, patted or cajoled into making the right response. The conditions necessary for us to learn in these circumstances will obviously be different.

If we were to examine the conditions for bringing about this higher type of learning, and we studied which methods paid dividends, we should come up with a number of hints as we did with our signal learning example. These would be the actual conditions necessary to bring about learning — how to teach people to do crosswords, fill in tax forms and suchlike.

How we arrive at five different types of learning

This brings us to an important point: the type of learning is defined by the conditions necessary to bring about that learning (Gagné 1977). Put simply it means that if a certain way of instructing brings about learning then that learning belongs to a particular type. For our purposes there are only five types of learning. 'Signal learning' we have already met in our example of the child and the radiator.

The kinds of learning which occur when crosswords are solved, or when new tax rules are followed, all involve fairly abstract ideas. The learning of ideas we call 'concept learning'. We will now examine the five types of learning starting with the easiest and most common.

(1) SIGNAL LEARNING

As already noted this kind of learning involves the learner in making a specific response to specific stimulus. Examples of signal learning in adults would be: when to use the 'scratch' and 'rumble' filters on high fidelity equipment; what to do when a warning light shows on a car instrument panel.

(2) CHAIN LEARNING

Chain learning involves the learner in being able to give a fixed, correct order to link a number of responses. The responses can either be verbal or physical. It is essential that the right sequence or chain of responses be followed; that the actions be performed in the right order.

Common examples of chain learning would include the following: starting a car; starting up or shutting down a boiler; building up a sentence in a foreign language; learning to play a tune on any instrument; calling up software.

You can see that in all these examples 'one thing leads to

another'. Learning how to do the task involves the learner in knowing just what comes next in the chain of events.

(3) MULTIPLE DISCRIMINATION LEARNING

Here the learner needs to be able to distinguish between situations or stimuli that are close together — close together, that is, in appearance or characteristics; the sort of learning that involves us in comparing similar phenomena, disentangling one from the other. Learning to adjust the colour balance on a TV set is an example. So is learning the intervals in musical chords, and learning to discriminate between different colours on litmus paper.

(4) CONCEPT LEARNING

This type of learning involves the learner in being able to make generalizations about objects or events; in finding common features and in labelling them. Learning for instance the ideas involved in 'bidding' in bridge or 'trumps' in whist. Other common examples are learning the concepts used in sport or recreation. On these occasions the learner very rapidly gets to learn new ideas relevant to the game: the concepts of 'snookering', 'back-spin', 'offside', to name a few.

(5) PRINCIPLE LEARNING

This learning requires the learner to link ideas together to form a principle or rule. It is clear that people cannot understand rules unless they can understand the ideas or concepts involved. For instance to understand the phrase 'all men are created equal' requires that we understand the idea of 'all men' and of 'equality'. So too with the rule: 'metals expand when heated'.

The kinds of learning which involve linking ideas that have previously been learned to form a principle or rule are found in the following situations: explaining to someone the principles of heat conservation and home insulation; learning new rules for deciding tax eligibility; learning the new ideas used in contemporary music.

How to instruct in the different types of learning

The example of signal learning demonstrated that there exist certain well-tried methods of instruction, of making sure that learning will take place. We managed to summarize these into four positive hints for instruction.

The real value of classifying learning into the five types lies in the fact that there are tried and tested methods for bringing about each type of learning. Each has its own appropriate set of methods just like our signal learning examples. These methods are given in Figure 7. Under signal learning we find the four points we noted earlier. As we read downwards we find the other four kinds of learning together with the appropriate hints. This is a tool to help you instruct which is going to be invaluable — you are going to be able to use the hints and tips in a wide variety of instructional settings.

How to analyse a task into type of learning

If we think of everyday instruction and consider the type of learning undertaken, something strikes us. It is that often we have a mixture of different types of learning. For example take someone learning how to start a car. He will be involved in signal learning — knowing the appropriate responses to the car controls. He needs to know also the correct chain of behaviour — a set sequence of checking the driving mirror, releasing the handbrake, signalling and so on. He might also be learning new ideas such as 'snatching' or 'slipping' the clutch.

In short, there will be a variety of types of learning in tasks that a learner is engaged in. This need be no problem for us. All the instructor has to do is to analyse the task and decide which kinds of learning predominate.

There might be only one predominant kind — more likely, though, there will be two or three. Examples of three common learning tasks analysed in this way are shown in Figure 8.

Hints for instruction appropriate for the type of learning

All we have to do, having identified the types of learning in the task, is to follow the appropriate hints for instruction. Let us see how this works in practice.

Suppose we are instructing someone in sawing by hand. First of all we have to ask ourselves a very basic question. Just what kinds of learning are we asking our novice to undertake?

As Figure 8 illustrates, the task of sawing involves three predominant types of learning — signal, chain and discrimination learning. Looking at Figure 7 we can easily use these

Signal learning

☐ Give easy-to-remember names for the stimulus — it helps learning.
☐ Show the stimulus and get the learner to respond correctly. Do this once or twice in succession.
☐ Strongly praise correct response.
☐ Plenty of practice fixes the learning.
☐ Spread the practice sessions out over time — it helps the learner.

Chain learning

☐ First make sure all the signals and correct responses are understood.
☐ Get the learner to speak out the links in the chain. For example trainee parachutists learn the procedure for opening their emergency parachute by repeating the following words: 'One: right hand hold parachute pack to chest. Two: left hand pull cord-ring and throw away. Three: left hand deep into parachute pack. Four: pull out parachute and throw far away.'
☐ Mnemonics help the learning of hard-to-remember chains. For example: Richard Of York Gave Battle In Vain (for the colours of the spectrum).
☐ Let the learner see the whole chain of events — to see how the links 'hang together'.
☐ Sometimes learning the chain backwards helps.
☐ Reassure the learner that it takes several attempts to learn a whole chain.

Multiple discrimination

☐ Distinguish distinctively what is to be discriminated: exaggerate, label or highlight it.
☐ Let the learner discriminate an 'easy' problem first then work progressively to harder discriminations.
☐ Plenty of practice with difficult examples helps.
☐ Spread the practice sessions out over time — it helps the learner remember.

Concept learning

☐ Can the idea be expressed symbolically or displayed diagrammatically? Be ready to try to express the ideas visibly with pencil, chalk or anything that lies to hand.
☐ Get the learner to generalize about the ideas.
☐ Be ready to try a variety of teaching procedures because repetition of ideas using the same words often does not work.
☐ Simply getting the learner to rehearse ideas parrot-fashion does not necessarily fix them in his mind. Get him to think and talk actively about the ideas and what they mean.
☐ Encourage the learner to look for both the similarities and differences between the new ideas and existing ideas.
☐ Always think out beforehand the essence of how concepts are being used and linked together. Emphasize this relationship. For example: is the essence of ideas that of inclusion? (A *and* B together.) Or exclusion? (*either* A *or* B, not both.) Or are they related? (*if* A *then* B.)

Principle learning

☐ A principle is either learned or it isn't — practice appears not to be important.
☐ Show how the concepts 'hang together' to form the principle.
☐ Always let the learner attempt to express the principle in his own language.
☐ Let the learner create his own examples of the principle.

Figure 7. *Types of learning and hints for instruction*

Type of Learning	Example 1 *Showing someone how to saw in a straight line*	Example 2 *Showing someone a new card game*	Example 3 *Showing someone 'starting off' procedure in a car*
Signal	Clear drawn line to be followed when cutting.	Can learner name the suits and values of the cards?	Car controls: can learner recognize what they mean? Does he know the appropriate responses?
Chain	Can learner establish a rhythm of cutting: pressure on forward stroke, less on return?	Is there an order of moves, or bids? Is there any set sequence to the game?	Starting chain: Check neutral Start Mirror Signal First gear Handbrake off Move off
Multiple discrimination	Can learner distinguish the correct angle of cutting? Can learner align the saw to the line by looking over the saw to the line?	Can learner understand the ranking of hands, e.g. the rank of hands in poker? Can he discriminate a 'good' hand from a 'bad' hand?	Can learner discriminate under-revving from over-revving? Can he discriminate 'bite' of clutch from non-engagement?
Concept		What are the major ideas involved? e.g. 'tricks', 'trumps', 'bids', etc.	'Snatching' the clutch; 'slipping' the clutch.
Principle		What is the overall goal of the game?	A smooth start fully under control.

Figure 8. *Types of learning in three tasks*

Learning to Teach Practical Skills

hints for our instruction. This is done for you in Figure 9. You will see that not all hints for each type of learning given in Figure 7 are used. We extract only those which are of obvious use for our example.

Type of Learning	Example	Instruction
Signal	Can the learner distinguish the drawn line?	'Can you see the line clearly? Remember to keep an eye on the line ahead of where you saw.'
	Can the learner start a cut correctly?	'To start the cut on the line, draw the saw gently upwards.'
Chain	Establish a rhythm of pressure on cutting stroke, less on return.	'The teeth of the saw are angled to cut on the downward stroke. They don't cut on the upward. Get a regular rhythm going.' (Demonstrate.)
Multiple discrimination	Distinguish and maintain the correct angle. Align the saw and line correctly.	'This is the correct angle (demonstrate). Not this, or this (exaggerated demonstration). As you saw, line up the saw with the line ahead of you.' (Demonstrate, let the learner see this.)

Figure 9. *Hints for instructing how to saw a straight line*

ANOTHER EXAMPLE

The final example of using the hints for instruction comes from paper-hanging.

As we all know, one of the trickiest parts of the art of paper-hanging is learning to transfer the pasted wall-paper from the paste table to the wall. Cutting out, marking up and measuring usually do not present too many difficulties. The fun starts at the pasting-up stage. Some of the sticky messes that absolute beginners get themselves into tell us it is definitely a skill with a 'knack' to it!

But let us now look more closely at what is required at this critical stage. The 'knack' consists simply in giving a little forethought to how the paper is picked up on the arm, and in going through a particular sequence of actions as the paper is placed on the wall.

Firstly the paper has to be folded neatly on the table so that it can be carried without danger of becoming unfolded. When it is presented to the wall, there is a tricky two-fold action.

78

Type of Learning	Example	Instruction
Signal	Recognize correctly folded paper on table	'Can you see the special way of folding, pasted-side to pasted-side? This stops it unfolding as you carry it.'
	Butting-in two lengths correctly	'See how you can press the two together or slide them apart if they overlap.'
Chain	1. Hold paper to wall at top. Butt in.	'Watch as I do these four stages. See how I hold the paper away from the wall until I am ready, in position.'
	2. Hold remainder of paper away from wall with other hand.	'Always work from the butt-join outwards.'
	3. Smooth paper to wall from the butt outwards.	'You will need a few trials before it comes easily.'
	4. Work downwards, introducing paper to the wall as needed.	'Don't despair!'
Multiple discrimination	Is the pattern joined up perfectly?	'Stand back. Can you see the join? Is there a jolt in the pattern?'
	Any trapped air bubbles? Wrinkles?	'Stand at a shallow angle to the wall. Can you see any bubbles?' (Show what one looks like.) 'Watch how bubbles or wrinkles show up when the light is at a shallow angle.'

Figure 10. *Hints for instruction in paper-hanging*

The top corner must be placed on the wall, butted-in correctly, and the remainder held off the wall with the other hand, to allow for positioning and 'slide'.

It sounds tricky, and it is. But once again let us analyse just what kinds of learning we are asking our novice to undertake. It is clear that the tricky sequence is an example of chain learning. But, looking more closely, we find several more types. This has been done for you in Figure 10. Here we have identified three kinds of learning. We have used the hints given in Figure 7 to guide our instruction.

TASK ANALYSIS: A TOOL TO HELP YOU

Clear, efficient instruction is simple if you follow these few rules:

☐ Stop. Think.

☐ Ask: 'What am I asking the learner to learn?'

☐ How many types of learning are involved?

☐ Turn to Figure 7.

☐ Use the hints appropriate for the type of learning.

Analysing the task (2): communicating and displaying the task

Often instruction is telling people how to undertake fairly large-scale projects or jobs which have within them a number of distinct stages. Often these stages have to be gone through in a particular order. Instructing someone in how to redesign and redecorate a room completely is one example. Showing someone how to site and plumb in a washing machine or how to plan, cook and serve a meal are other common examples.

In this second section we look at a different way of analysing tasks. Instead of breaking down what is to be learned into the kinds of learning, we look closely at the various parts of the task, and how they logically hold together. We look at how useful it is to be able to explain clearly the relationship of all the parts of the task. This is a time-tried method used for making decisions in industry. As one can imagine, the problem of training personnel in operating an oil refinery plant or power-station will be enormous. The same method is used, however, for these large-scale training design problems as our own humble everyday examples. The same basic principles apply. These are:

1. Defining what the overall objectives are.
2. Talking about objectives with the learner.
3. Showing the learner the structure of the task.

What are the overall objectives of the task?

What overriding goal should govern every move, thought or action as the learner does the job?

How many times have I heard instructors give instruction without giving this basic knowledge to the learner! It is so simple, yet so easily overlooked. The reason is that when we do jobs ourselves we forget the importance of the overall objectives. We know them of course, but we don't need to voice them, to spell them out. They have become second nature, not needing to be voiced openly. An example will illustrate this.

INSTRUCTION: THE NEED FOR OBJECTIVES

A mother, herself a keen cyclist, was teaching her young daughter how to ride her new ten-speed cycle. They went for a short spin together round their neighbourhood. Progress was slow, the girl repeatedly 'crashed' the gears; was in the wrong gear at the wrong time; was struggling up hills in top gear and frantically pedalling for all she was worth going down. Finally they stopped.

The mother was thoughtful. She had spent a great deal of time before they set off explaining how the gears worked and how to change them gently. Yet it was apparent that there was something fundamentally wrong with her daughter's approach to the machine.

That was it! So concerned had she been with the details of the gears that she had forgotten to explain why you had gears in the first place. She realized that she had missed out the most important part of her explanation.

'I've forgotten to explain something. The whole point about riding a ten-speed bike is that using the gears properly should allow you to keep the same rate rate of pedalling. One — two — one — two — one — two — a bit faster or slower, whichever suits your body best. Now the golden rule is to keep the same rhythm going no matter whether you are going uphill or downhill. This is because you pedal most efficiently using your energy evenly. No slow straining or whizzing round frantically like you've been doing. Your gears allow you to do this; the trick is to use them thoughtfully. If you see a slight incline ahead you know you will slow up, so you get ready to change down beforehand. Similarly when you are over the top of a hill and start to speed up on your way down, you change to a higher gear.'

USEFUL TIPS

☐ When instructing ask yourself what the overall guiding objective of the task is.

☐ Try to explain principles and objectives as simply and clearly as possible.

☐ Remember that the overall objective is the 'master-plan' of the activity; it serves to guide the learner.

Talking about objectives with the learner

In the previous example of learning to ride a cycle the overall objectives can be said to be fairly cut and dried. There are tasks of course where the overall objectives are not so clear cut; where people's preferences, tastes or values are involved. Examples would be decorating, much handcraft work, or any project involving personal taste.

In these cases how can an instructor talk about the guiding principles involved in objectives, when the objectives have yet to be decided?

It is here that the instructor has to talk carefully with the learner, to point out all the possible kinds of objectives and to decide on a suitable one together. It has to be a really meaningful dialogue, not a hurried question and answer. In the following example note how the instructor explains the possible range of objectives from which the learner can choose. He is careful to make sure that he does not decide for him. He is careful to avoid influencing the learner's choice too much. What is clear is that the learner appreciates deciding on suitable overall objectives. Because he has a hand in defining what the target is going to be, motivation to reach the target will be high.

INSTRUCTION: DECIDING ON OBJECTIVES TOGETHER

Instructor: 'When you make plans to redesign a room it is best first to consider the physical features of the room. These you can do very little about. Without

	spending a lot of money you cannot alter the position of the door, the window, the plumbing and so on.'
Learner:	'Yes, or that chimney breast over there, or this alcove (pointing). But I like the long shape of the room with the window at the end.'
Instructor:	'Do you want to emphasize the room's shape and the light coming in?'
Learner:	'I don't know, how can I do it?'
Instructor:	'To take two extremes: you can either have the room in darkish colours to get a warm and cosy effect, or you might want something brighter, more airy, more open.'
Learner:	'I think I prefer something small and cosy-feeling — lots of junk and furniture.'
Instructor:	'Yet this room has a lot of uses ...'
Learner:	'Yes, it's got to serve as a study, have my desk and books in — as well as entertaining and sleeping in.'
Instructor:	'You can either think about using different areas for different things, like having a work area over there (points) and eating and listening to records, for instance, here.
	Alternatively, you can let the same area have different uses. Have a worktop here, for instance. Yet have it portable to be taken away when you have your friends round. Similarly with the bed. You can have one that folds flat against the wall ...'
Learner:	'I rather like the idea of little areas for different purposes.'
Instructor:	'Right. Now let's think what features of the room best serve your different purposes. First the light ...'

USEFUL TIPS

☐ When deciding together on objectives try to present the alternatives as fairly as possible. Let the learner decide.

☐ Don't make up the learner's mind for him!

☐ Involve the learner at every decision point. Let him pick and choose.

☐ Help him to formulate realistic objectives in as clear, understandable terms as possible. Avoid vague phrases.

Showing the learner the structure of the task

We have now talked with our learner about the overall objectives of the job. Where necessary we have involved him in decisions. In short, we know clearly where we are going, the goal is precisely stated. But how do we get there?

The subject of this section is communicating to the learner the various parts or stages of the job. Most complex jobs, as we have noted, have a number of distinct phases to them. Although it is perfectly clear to a skilled performer how the various parts make up the whole, this doesn't apply to the learner. We must remember that he very often knows nothing about how the task is made up.

Most everyday tasks can be described in a set of sub-goals which have to be reached before we can get to the final objective. For example in our decorating illustration, before the learner can attain the overall objective of a redesigned room he might have to strip and prepare the walls and he might even have to do some electrical rewiring. These are sub-goals.

To be able to convey to the learner that there is a particular order of sub-goals to be reached before the overall objective is the hallmark of a good instructor.

Let us suppose we are instructing someone in how to make a hot cup of tea. This involves the sub-goals of bringing the water to the boil; preparing and warming the teapot; measuring out tea, sugar, milk. All these sub-goals we would agree contribute to the overall objective of a good cup of tea. If we display this diagrammatically we have four distinct stages as shown in Figure 11.

What we have to do is decide what are the most important priorities in the task of making tea; each must be gone through systematically. If we analyse tasks in this way and present simple diagrams to the learner they can be of enormous help. They are maps to guide the learner.

Let us now take a rather more complicated example. Suppose we want to explain to someone the rather tricky process of making an appetizing omelette. As any omelette-maker knows, here is a task which needs approaching in a methodical manner. Poor preparation and you end up with a sticky mess! Figure 12 shows how it is done.

Again the same principles apply: break down the task into the basic elements that make up the job. In this case we can see four distinct parts to cooking an omelette: getting

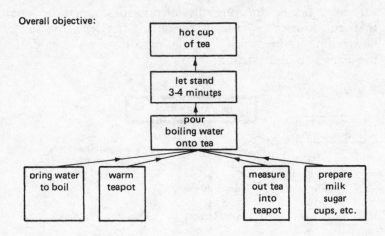

Figure 11. *Task analysis: making tea*

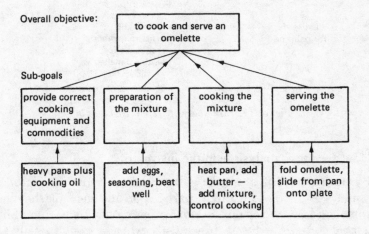

Figure 12. *Task analysis: making an omelette*
(after Duncan 1972)

together the right cooking utensils, preparing the mixture, cooking the mixture and finally serving the omelette. Each of these four parts is made up of other parts, and so on.

Our final example is taken from a decorating job. Assume we have a rather weatherbeaten old door, a little the worse

85

for wear. Let us draw up a list of priorities, a plan of action that our learner can use in repainting it. Here, by way of illustration is the task of repainting a door represented for the learner to understand.

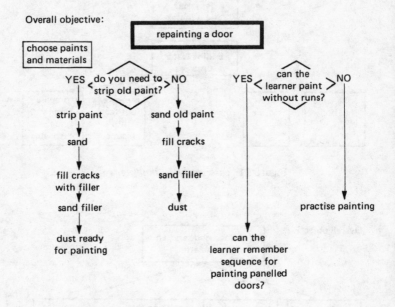

Figure 13. *Task analysis: repainting a door*

How does task analysis help the instructor?

By having to display all the parts of the task the instructor is reminded of those various parts. For instance in showing someone how to repaint a door we may omit to ask him if he is able to paint without 'runs'. Only when he comes finally to paint might it become apparent — clearly not the best time for the instructor to find this out! By doing a simple task analysis we are forced into thinking about the relevance of all parts of a task. Displaying the task gives the learner something concrete and real to work to, for it supplies him with a useful 'map' of the project ahead. He can see where he is, where he is going, how far he has to go. A clearly displayed task analysis helps in other ways too. It stops the instructor trying to explain too much with words, getting tied down with lengthy explanations.

One clearly displayed task analysis saves a thousand words!

Using both types of analysis

Instructing fairly large jobs such as decorating, assembly or repair jobs is helped by task analysis. The set sequences or links in the procedure are made clear and the flow chart or diagram drawn should show a clear representation to both the instructor and learner.

Having reached this point we can go further in our analysis, for we can analyse the actual kinds of learning required to undertake each of the identified sub-goals and stages. This was the process of analysing learning described first in this chapter. If often happens that single identifiable skills occur as components of large procedures. We can illustrate how this is done by reconsidering Figure 13. Looking more closely at the various sub-goals involved in the overall task we can see that applying the filler to cracks and scratches prior to painting would definitely involve the learner in particular types of learning. A particular type of skill is needed. It lies embedded in the overall task in the same way that the particular skill of making a tennis serve lies within the game of tennis. In learning to apply filler effectively the learner would have to develop careful visual discriminations and also to learn a simple chain. Therefore when we come to instruct at this point in the task we must recognize that we are asking the learner to undertake two very different kinds of learning. Using Figure 7, our instruction would include the following:

CHAIN LEARNING INVOLVED IN MIXING AND APPLYING FILLER:

The stages must be demonstrated in the right order:

1. After sanding-down estimate volume of filler that is needed.
2. Mix the filler (NB make sure learner can discriminate the right consistency).
3. Apply the filler, smooth off.
4. Let dry.
5. Smooth off with sandpaper.

DISCRIMINATION LEARNING INVOLVED IN FILLING:

First show examples of fine cracks or deformities in the existing paintwork that a new coat of paint will easily conceal. These would then be contrasted with examples obviously severe enough to need filling. Successively closer examples would be found and explained to the learner.

Using the same procedure we can see that the sub-goal of painting by hand involves certain types of learning. It is predominantly a chain learning activity, but some discrimination learning is also involved:

CHAIN LEARNING INVOLVED IN PAINTING:

1. Hold the brush correctly.
2. Don't overload the brush (avoid dipping in paint more than one quarter depth of brush).
3. Lightly touch insides of paint can with loaded brush to remove excess paint.
4. Holding brush downwards, quickly transfer brush to surface.
5. Demonstrate smooth up-down motion transferring paint evenly on to the surface.
6. Make sure the correct angle of brush strokes is maintained by supple wrist action.
7. Demonstrate final light brush stroke to ensure no brush marks are left.

DISCRIMINATION LEARNING INVOLVED IN PAINTING:

1. Demonstrate under-application of paint contrasted with over-application and their consequences.
2. Demonstrate how to find a viewpoint so that the light reveals runs developing. Point to examples.
3. Alert the learner to danger spots for runs. Show examples of hairs, dust, etc, on wet surface and how to remove them and over-paint.

Conclusion

This chapter has looked at two ways in which we can prepare and organize our instruction. We can first find out the kinds of learning we are asking our learner to undertake, then we can select appropriate hints for instruction. If a fairly large-scale task is involved we could break it down into its components and display these so as to show how the parts make up the whole.

The two methods can profitably be used together; particular

skills involving particular kinds of learning are often encountered within large tasks.

Finally, no job is too large or complicated, no skill too small or trivial not to benefit by being analysed. It can only result in a clearer conception of what is involved both for the instructor and subsequently for the learner. Whether you are instructing someone in the skill of changing a baby's nappy or changing a car engine, proper task analysis lays the foundation for successful instruction.

References

Duncan, K (1972) Strategies for analysis of the task. In Hartley, J (ed) *Strategies for Programmed Instruction*. Butterworths, London.

Gagné, R M (1977) *The Conditions of Learning* (3rd edition). Holt, Rinehart & Winston, New York.

Further Reading

Annett, J, Duncan, K D, Stammers, R B and Gray, M J (1971) *Task Analysis*. HMSO, London.

Davies, I K (1971) *The Management of Learning*. McGraw-Hill, London.

Davies, I K (1973) *The Organisation of Training*. McGraw-Hill, London.

Davies, I K (1976) *Objectives in Curriculum Design*. McGraw-Hill, London.

Hartley, J and Davies, I K (1976) Pre-instructional Strategies: The Role of Pretests, Behavioural Objectives, Overviews and Advance Organisers. *Review of Educational Research*, Spring, 46, 2, 239-265.

Popham, W J and Baker, E C (1970) *Systematic Instruction*. Prentice-Hall, New Jersey.

Singer, R N (1972) *Readings in Motor Learning*. Lea & Febiger, Philadelphia.

Chapter 6
During instruction

> **Overview:** This chapter examines the communication that takes
> place between the instructor and learner during the period of
> instruction. It examines when to talk and when not to talk, when
> to explain and offer guidance, how to encourage learners to
> learn, and how to build their confidence in their learning abilities.
> Some common errors of instruction are shown by examples, and
> the chapter gives tips for making instruction more effective and
> rewarding.

Introduction

It is hoped that the previous chapters will have made us
aware of the need for careful preparation before beginning
instruction. We will, by now, be familiar with the main senses
being used in skills together with their four-fold nature: the
input of the senses; the decision process of the brain; the
output of bodily actions; and feedback. Our 'instructional
homework' will have been done too — we will know something about the kind of learning we are asking the learner to
engage in, and we will have some idea as to how to go about
instructing in it. Finally, if the task we are explaining is a
complex multi-stage one, we will begin to break the task
down, analysing the logic of it in order to simplify and explain
it the more easily to the learner.

All this has been done with only passing reference to the
most important person in learning — the learner! He is undoubtedly the most important, the most complicated and the
most unpredictable part of the whole process! It is essential
that when we start instructing we start off on the right footing.
Let us clear away any misconceptions we may have about
learners before we begin.

The special nature of instruction

Communication takes place between people. We use words
and gestures to communicate to one another. Miscommunication can occur when people don't listen to messages; when
we mispronounce words, use the wrong ones or don't hear the

message that is given; when we hear instead the message we would like to hear.

All these errors arise because we are human, fallible and error-prone. Yet we accept this miscommunication. We ask each other to repeat words or phrases when we are not attending; we are hurt by the misinterpreted phrase; we take offence at what we interpret as 'hidden meaning' of messages. In short the consequences of miscommunication in social settings are many; offence, indifference, humour — even anger.

Why is instruction special?

Instruction, however, is a special kind of communication. The consequences of miscommunication in instruction are just as real as social miscommunication — one might even maintain that they are felt the more keenly! The consequences of poorly managed and poorly communicated instruction are confusion, disappointment, and even downright despair on the part of the learner — and a damaged relationship between the learner and instructor.

Instruction is a unique form of social interaction. It involves a transaction between humans: something is offered, and something is taken. Above all, the little piece of social drama called 'instruction' requires tact and sensitivity in order to handle it well.

The old-fashioned romantic view was that good teachers and instructors were 'born and not made'. They either possessed the tact and sensitivity to do it well, or they did not. No amount of training, it used to be believed, could make a bad teacher or instructor into a better one.

Because instructional psychology is now becoming increasingly conversant with the intricacies of instruction it is possible to offer a few simple rules to aid the novice instructor. By following them you will not necessarily become an expert overnight — only practice and experience will bring that. What we can do is offer a guide to the right techniques, what pitfalls to avoid.

Rule 1. Beware of imitating! Be yourself!

All of us have had experience of instructing someone, of demonstrating or 'showing how'. We do it unknowingly almost every day. Most of the time we are not even conscious that we are engaged in teaching or instruction.

However, the moment we are asked to approach instruction in a professional manner, or to engage in a large-scale piece of instruction, what happens to us?

Evidence from industrial research is illuminating here, for studies of experienced manual workers 'made up' to instructors (Department of Employment 1969) show that workers model themselves upon those who in turn instructed them. Lacking guidance in a new situation the would-be instructors — like all humans — look for persons to imitate; look for a model of behaviour which they can copy easily for themselves. Not surprisingly these new found instructors took the model that was nearest to hand. They imitated, as faithfully as possible, those instructors who had previously taught them!

The dangers of this process are clear: the moral for our instruction clearer still. It is that imitation can be dangerous and should be avoided. The golden rule is 'be yourself'. Try not to model yourself on our favourite teacher or instructor or your favourite television hero. It won't work!

Countless times have I seen persons whose behaviour in non-instructional settings is perfectly natural and free, suddenly change when they are asked to instruct. They put on the most strange and unnatural ways.

What do they do? They might suddenly adopt a haughty, offputting manner, excessively authoritarian and demanding. Equally upsetting, they might become over-familiar and condescending. All they are doing is calling up the ghost of their ideal instructor, whoever that may be.

Of course the effect on the learner is obvious. He senses false behaviour quickly, he rapidly notices play-acting. The spontaneous person he knew suddenly becomes someone else, someone alien, someone unknown. Not being used to this 'new' person he stops learning from him. In these cases instruction is doomed before it has even begun.

To conclude, if you find yourself slipping into imitating the ways and mannerisms of someone else, stop instructing! Change the subject, move away from the physical area where you are instructing, taking your learner with you. Have a talk about the weather, sport, hobbies or anything. Begin to react naturally with him once again. Let your own personality shine through. It's the best you've got!

Rule 2. Inspire confidence: start with the learner

All of us carry at least one set of fond memories of our own experiences while being instructed. The memories are intensely personal, intimate and often treasured and untold to others. Think about them for a moment.

They might be memories of a friend, a lover or a spouse lovingly sharing a skill with us. They might be memories of respected teachers or instructors long ago, whose methodical explanations we can still remember today. Our memories might be even more fresh: for instance remembering recent instruction where we have been excited by the discovery of hidden abilities within ourselves, or where we have been inspired to learn more by an instructor who has fired our imagination.

OUR FEELINGS

Without doubt the overriding feeling was one of confidence in ourselves. The sure, methodical descriptions offered by the instructor were given to us in a warm, secure atmosphere. We were free to make mistakes, we could fail miserably in our attempts, we could look and sound ridiculous.

Always though, we were accepted, errors and all, by the instructor. When we took our first unsteady steps in the newly-acquired skill his guidance, his helpful words were never threatening to us, never destructive to our confidence. The quality of the relationship, the warm, accepting, learning atmosphere was directly responsible for our confidence.

In short, it was an atmosphere which provided for personal growth, which allowed us to develop, learn from our mistakes, somehow grow in stature.

How can you as an instructor inspire confidence in the learner?

HOW TO GET CONFIDENCE

It is done simply by making the learner the foundation-stone for all your actions and all your explanations. By this is meant the deliberate attempt by you, the instructor, to start with the actual abilities, faults and needs of the learner — and not with what you expect them to have!

To base your instruction on the learner's needs is easy. First find out carefully what the learner already knows about the subject or skill in question. Find out what he feels about things. Find out what ideas he has about what he is to learn. Ask him what he already knows, even before you begin instructing.

True, this can only be done with a certain amount of effort on the part of the instructor, for it means entering into a real person-to-person dialogue with the learner. By this we do not mean going through the motions of a quick 'sounding out' of what he knows. No hurried chats or clipped question-and-answer sessions are going to reveal what we are looking for.

We need instead a genuine two-way communication between instructor and learner. Offer support, offer help. Never hurry or upset the learner at this stage. Be as patient and thorough as is humanly possible. Remember you are setting the scene for the whole period of instruction to follow. In the example below the instructor is clarifying how much the learner knows about the subject. Notice how she gets the response of the learner, how she gets her involved right from the beginning in objectives for learning. Notice especially how the instructor is careful to base everything she does and says on what the learner can actually do, for this is going to serve as the basis for everything later on.

AN EXAMPLE: LEARNER-CENTRED INSTRUCTION TO BUILD
CONFIDENCE (taken from audio-tape)

Instructor: (teaching dressmaking) 'Have you had any experience before?'

Learner: 'Yes, a little.'

Instructor: 'What did you make, would you like to tell me?'

Learner: 'A dress, using a very simple pattern.'

Instructor: 'Could you tell me if it included "gathering", "darts" or collars or anything more complicated?'

Learner: 'I did some gathering, putting in a zip, but I had lots of difficulty putting in the collar and fixing the sleeves . . .'

Instructor: 'So you would say you are happy about most of the basics: cutting out, seams and darts?'

Learner: 'Yes . . . but I need help on the more difficult, fiddly things.'

Instructor: 'What do you see as fiddly or difficult? Can you tell me what they are?'

Learner:	'Putting in waistbands, the bodice, and that sort of thing.'
Instructor:	'Tell me if this idea suits you. I'll start first with going over simple darts, then we'll go on to gathering, waistbands and such like.'
Learner:	'Yes, that's fine ... (pause) ... but there's something very basic that I haven't grasped. I'd like to go over that as well.'
Instructor:	'Oh, what's that? We'll go over that too ...'

Instructors often base their instruction on how they themselves have previously acquired and developed a particular skill. As soon as they start instructing they are thinking and talking, not as they should be about their learner and how he is going to learn, but about their *own* past experience. They base instruction upon themselves:

'I learnt it like this ...'
'This is the way I was taught how to do it ...'
'It's always been taught this way ...'
'I started off learning it like this ...'

Phrases such as these at the beginning of instruction are dangerous and offputting. They show that the instructor is not concentrating on the learner, his values and his needs. Instruction is becoming based on the instructor rather than on the learner.

BEWARE OF THE TRAP

It is so easy to fall into the trap of instructor-centred instruction because we ourselves forget what it is like to be a learner, especially if we are instructing in a skill which we first learned a long time ago. We have forgotten what it is like to be a learner, we have forgotten the simple rules of learning, we have forgotten the stumbling blocks that so easily upset and unbalance the beginner.

This quality of being near to the learner, of making instruction learner-centred, comes naturally to people who have only just acquired a skill themselves and are then called upon to instruct someone else in it.

Children who have just learnt to read and are then showing younger playmates or brothers and sisters are a good example. Indeed any persons who have newly acquired a skill often make excellent instructors themselves in that skill. Why should this be so? It is because they approach their instruction through the eyes of the learner. They can easily remember what it was like. They have not been told that there is a right way or a wrong way of instructing, consequently everything they do and say is based on the learner's needs.

Some convincing evidence of the value of basing instruction on the learner comes from research on driving instructors conducted in a public transport driving school (Belbin & Belbin 1972).

A group of instructors was selected who had a high pass-rate of getting learners through the Public Service Vehicle Test. Less successful instructors were also selected (those who managed to get fewer through the test). The two groups were then interviewed about how they approached their instruction.

The more successful instructors appeared to be especially concerned with their students — they were continually looking for student reaction to instruction and were on the lookout for learner problems. They also said that they would try to 'mould' their instruction to cope with particular problems of trainees.

Less successful instructors, however, operated in a different manner: for a start they were more concerned with the formal requirements of instruction and the demands they made on the learners. They also wanted to talk more about how they themselves had learned to drive.

To start effective instruction we need the co-operation and confidence of learners. We can gain this by basing our instruction on them as individuals; on their abilities and knowledge, and their needs as learners.

To a certain extent we can see a contradiction to what was said in the previous chapter. The astute instructor reading Chapter 5 may have prepared a careful list of goals and subgoals contained in the learning task. He might be ready to instruct in what he considers to be a logical sequence as dictated by the nature of the task.

What we now say is that this plan should never strait-jacket our dealings with the learner. Plans should serve only loosely to organize our instruction, never render it inflexible, rulebound. The guiding principle appears to be this: the learner seems to learn better by his own 'route' through instruction and we should be prepared to follow the learner's direction.

Always be prepared to base instruction on the unique needs of your learner (Mager and Clark 1963, Mager 1972).

But how is this done in practice?

It is done by careful assessment of the learner's existing abilities and knowledge. This need not be as daunting as it sounds, for it merely involves us in carefully examining what he can do already and in listening attentively to what he says. We can often see for ourselves how much skill and experience a learner already has — if he can already manipulate his fingers for keyboard skills; if he knows the correct way to pick up and hold a hand tool, for instance.

Once they have clear goals set out, adult learners are often the best judges of what they need to add to their knowledge. Most learners are likely to know something, no matter how trivial, about what they are going to learn. It is always up to the instructor to ask them, to get them to talk, to relate what they know about the skill. True, they might have misconceptions about the skill in question, they might easily have the wrong ideas about how to learn — but all this is still of value to the instructor. The main point is that as well as giving the learner a useful say in the activity of learning it also supplies the instructor with information as to where to begin, what routes to suggest through the learning task. This is the essence of what the dressmaking instructress was doing in the previous example.

Instruction should always start at the edge of the learner's knowledge. It should not necessarily go over routes already travelled or, for that matter, start from a point too far ahead for the learner to understand.

Rule 3. Get in tune with the learner

From research on phenomenally successful instructors, we learn that as a breed they are especially sensitive to people. They seem to be able to empathize or understand the feelings of their students. They do this often in uncanny ways. Below are some tape-recorded comments made by adults talking about their instructors. It is revealing to hear how they describe their instructors.

Male, 19, speaking of an acquaintance who taught him rock-climbing techniques: 'Looking back over time he exposed me to progressively harder grades of climb in a way that suited me perfectly . . . he never once overstretched me, or took me beyond my limits so that I became scared or dispirited. Yet each time I went with him he would give me some new goal to conquer — always, with a degree of effort, just within my capabilities . . . It was uncanny how he judged my limits, but he seemed to know just how I felt . . . it was almost as if he could get right inside my muscles and understand how I felt. I never could understand how he did it . . .'

Female, 21, speaking of someone who taught her musical notation and harmony for guitar: 'He'd explain, demonstrate, then explain some more. Like that. When things became a bit more advanced he'd explain some point, illustrate it by playing, then ask me if I understood. Strange, but he often didn't even bother to ask me if I had grasped the point. Instead he would glance up rapidly from the guitar and look at me quickly. And he knew of course, just by this rapid glance, if I'd understood the point or not . . .'

WHAT ARE SUCCESSFUL INSTRUCTORS DOING?

These examples suggest that the effective instructor is exceptionally clever at reading and understanding the subtle signals that the learner gives during instruction. He is noticing and interpreting all the minute behaviours and 'body-language' given out by the learner. He notices all the nods, the despairing sighs, the half-frown of incomprehension, the clouded eyes of lack of understanding, the slight change in posture signalling incipient fatigue — all these and a thousand more messages, are noticed by the alert instructor.

Although controversy surrounds whether you can actually train instructors (or anybody for that matter) to be sensitive to people's behaviour, to be able to empathize (Smith, H C 1966, Smith, P B 1974), there are nevertheless a number of points you, the instructor, can usefully ask yourself in order to help you understand the behaviour of your learner.

TIPS TO HELP UNDERSTAND THE LEARNER

☐ Are you familiar with the learner's habitual ways of behaving? Do you know how to 'read' him, how he expresses his feelings? Do you know the language he uses to convey his feelings, thoughts and emotions? Try to note how he conveys these and be on the lookout for them during instruction, for it will help you get on his wave-length quickly.

TIPS TO HELP UNDERSTAND THE LEARNER *(continued)*

☐ Do you have any preconceptions about the learner which might potentially damage his learning? Do you, for instance, see him as a 'rapid learner' or a 'slow learner'? Forget these ideas. Remember that the rate of learning is specific to a particular task and is not a general ability that applies to all tasks. Always be ready for some surprises!

☐ In your dealings with the learner, are you seeing him in terms of an inappropriate stereotype and not as a genuine individual? Are you seeing him just as an example of a particular 'type' of person? Don't do this. It is always unfair to him as an individual.

☐ Have you established a good working relationship based on mutual respect? Have you established rapport with the learner? Does he speak freely with you? Does he freely admit mistakes to you in an uninhibited way? Can you laugh and joke together about the whole learning process?

Rule 4. When you are emotionally involved with the learner — be careful!

Frequently instruction is between people who have varying degrees of emotional involvement. These might be friends, acquaintances, lovers, neighbours or flatmates. Emotional involvement between instructor and learner unfortunately can often work against successful instruction. Most of us can relate disaster stories of failed instruction undertaken with our loved ones. 'Husband-teaching-wife-to-drive' is the common cartoon cliché.

Before we analyse what element it is in a strong emotional involvement that so often works against successful instruction, we have first to examine the nature of the social relationship between teacher and learner.

In formal learning environments — schools, colleges and paid tuition, for example — the relationship between teacher and taught is instrumental. By this we mean the teacher is a means to the learner acquiring a particular end. Failure to learn in these formal situations is often rationalized in terms of the other's performance. For example teachers grumble of 'falling pupil standards', 'pupil inattentiveness' and so on. In turn, learners question 'inadequate instruction', the syllabus' or 'the system'.

Failure to learn in these situations is rarely seen as self-failure. It is almost as if the distance between teacher and taught structures and controls criticism itself, for criticism is often about objects — buildings, finance, curriculum and suchlike.

This is not so when there is intense involvement between learner and teacher. These situations we shall term 'affective relationships'.

WHAT GOES WRONG?

Here failure to learn breeds no such controlled criticism easily passed on to something — or someone — else. Failure is painful self-failure on the part of the learner. In the heady atmosphere of emotional involvment criticism of each other rapidly spills over to include criticism of each other's personal qualities. Often heated arguments follow, in which the basis of the whole relationship is questioned. It is sad, but unfortunately true.

In this way many an otherwise beautiful relationship witnesses the beginning of the end when one person attempts to instruct the other.

Exhortations for both learner and instructor to become less emotional with one another when in these instructional situations mean little, once the heady spiral of damaged feelings and barbed criticism has started. Things all too rapidly boil over.

When you do find yourself instructing someone who is emotionally cose to you, you can guard against possible disaster by following the points below:

TIPS FOR INSTRUCTION

☐ You know the signs your partner shows when he or she is hurt or angry. You yourself know the time scale involved when an eruption or outburst is on the way.

☐ Stop instructing as soon as this build-up starts. Change activity, or rest. Space your instruction out over time. Take a break, put on a record. Do anything! Don't attempt an intensive long session for you are courting disaster!

☐ Never, when faced with failure or error on the part of your partner, use it as an occasion for mentioning outstanding grievances or disputes. Never use learning failure as an excuse to criticize your relationship. Do it another time, in another place.

TIPS FOR INSTRUCTION *(continued)*

☐ Attempt to keep all comment strictly related to what is being undertaken in instruction. Try and build an atmosphere of calm or civility.

☐ Never attempt generalizations about your partner, for example by saying: 'That's just like you to do that.' In doing this you are bringing in the other roles that he/she may have. Keep those other roles out of it. Just concentrate on immediate performance, the here-and-now.

☐ Remember that criticism is felt extremely keenly in emotionally-involved relationships. Partners are hypersenstive to criticism, and offence is therefore correspondingly easier to achieve. For this reason pay particular attention to the value of praise (Rule 7).

Rule 5. Carefully explain objectives

Spoken or written directions typically form the early directions given by the instructor or the learner. Over-zealous instructors, keen to give their learners the correct guidance, will always talk too much in the early stages of training. They 'submerge' their learners in over-long instructions. This is a finding to emerge from studies of novice instructors (ITRU 1975).

If instruction is to be effective it should be neither too elaborate nor too abstract. Simple, practical directions give the best results. There are of course exceptions to this rule, both of which we have already dealt with. These need to be briefly reviewed.

The first exception is that words may actually be useful in learning chains of behaviour (Chapter 5). In this case the use of carefully selected words to 'label' behaviour in order to help the learner remember sequences is of especial value. 'Mirror, signal, select gear' is such a case.

The second exception is where the instructor may find that a few well chosen words are particularly evocative of the phenomenon to be explained. For instance words may serve to cue the learner into making subtle perceptual distinctions. 'Slightly fogged' is a phrase used to describe off-white or slightly exposed printing paper. Another example is 'souriant' — literally 'smiling'. This refers to the stage of cooking of stew or soup just before it simmers when the surface film of the dish ripples or creases into a 'smile'. Notice how words such as these use careful, even off-beat analogy to achieve their effect. The learner, grasping their meaning, can really begin to make fine, precise discriminations.

SHORT EXPLANATIONS OF OBJECTIVES ARE BEST

Apart from these two exceptions, all instructors are advised to avoid weighty, wordy explanations and instructions. For simple, practical instruction, resist the temptation to use your voice too much. Do not attempt to deliver mini-lectures or use fancy, impressive sounding phrases. This is the surest way to lose the attention of the learner.

Typical errors of a novice instructor (and many not-so-novice instructors) are as follows. They ramble on needlessly. They repeat themselves. They give long formidable lists of don'ts — 'Don't do this!' 'Don't do that!' 'Never do this.'

Worst of all for the learner, instructors' sentences often become long and complicated; difficult to follow; cloudy and unclear. The best way to illustrate this is by example. Below is one instructor making just these kinds of errors. He is explaining the objectives of stripping paint using a blowlamp and scraper.

THE ERROR OF UNNECESSARILY COMPLICATED INSTRUCTION

'Be careful here because if you scorch the wood you have damaged it for ever — that is if you are going to want to varnish it or something. Of course if you are going to paint it, it doesn't matter. But anyway scorching is never caused by keeping the flame moving. Instead it is done when the blowlamp is kept on one spot. Watch me.

See, it's just like peeling paint after it has bubbled up when you use a chemical paint stripper. But first you have to get the paint hot, like this. No, I mean before that you have to wave it over the paint. Be careful of the hot scrapings falling down, they are red hot. Which reminds me, you can test to see if the paint is softening up by using your scraper. When you stick at it long enough you will be able to do it like this.

Here, your turn now...'

103

PRACTICAL HINTS FOR EXPLANATIONS

☐ Keep spoken sentences short. Never use long, complicated ones. If you think of what you mean to say in short clear sentences, you will not fall into the trap of speaking in long convoluted ones.

☐ Always use words and names you are absolutely sure the learner understands.

☐ Make sure the ideas you use are known and are familiar to the learner.

☐ Learners always grasp affirmative, positive statements better than negative ones.

☐ It is often easy to stimulate learner interest by using pronouns.

☐ You always want your instructions and objectives to ring in the ears of your learner as he attempts the task. You want him to remember them. Strike a hopeful note! Inspire confidence.

Research into making explanation and instruction easily understood by the learner gives us clear guidelines (Hartley 1985). We can use these for any kind of instruction — whether it is long and involved, or simple and short. The rules are the same.

If the instructor in the paint stripping example had used the above guide lines we should hear him instructing like this:

'This paint softens when it is warmed by the blowlamp flame. You can then scrape it off easily. Watch closely. (Demonstrates.) Hold your lamp and blade together just off the wood. Wave the flame on the paint to soften it.

Point your flame off the wood. Hold it there and with your other hand scrape. One bit at a time.

You'll soon pick it up. Here, have a go.'

Rule 6. Explain — then demonstrate!

After we have carefully explained the objectives for learning, instruction usually takes a practical turn. The instructor will accompany instruction with a practical, live demonstration. This may take many forms: say, of some particular action in sport, or of tool-use or of equipment-use.

It should never be forgotten that this initial demonstration is of tremendous value to the learner. Most likely it will be the first time he has seen the full-scale activity or skill at such close quarters. Since it is performed solely for his benefit, and he is honoured with a grandstand view, he is usually more than eager to learn all there is to know.

At this point the careful instructor will be using the principle of selectively 'cueing' the learner into attending to the correct sense channel. He will also pay attention to 'feedback' of information so that the learner can understand how he is progressing. And so the demonstration begins.

It is at this stage that, again, traps lie for the unwary instructor. The over-zealous instructor often attempts too much, usually by talking while demonstrating. He forgets that the skill being demonstrated is packed full of astounding interest for the learner. It is, after all being demonstrated for his sole interest and enjoyment. I see many instructors forget or ignore the impact of this first demonstration on the learner. After all, the skill being demonstrated is an everyday occurence. It is something practised and almost second nature to the instructor.

A COMMON FAULT

In short as instructors they have forgotten to keep a weathereye on the learner, to imagine what the learner is experiencing. A typical mistake for the instructor would be to 'talk over' the demonstration; to attempt to deliver lengthy explanations; to give too many tips, altogether too much detail while demonstrating. Most, if not all, of this usually goes straight over the learner's head, because his attention is riveted by what is going on before him. Why should this be so?

For the answer we must look at an idea discussed earlier in Chapter 3. Humans have a strictly limited capacity for attending to information. They cannot both watch something carefully with the whole of their attention *and* attend to heavyweight verbal instructions at the same time. Evidence from research on instruction seems to suggest (Anderson 1969, Hsia 1971) that there is little to be gained by 'flooding' all the learner's communication channels.

The golden rule is always to keep your instruction simple when it is accompanied by demonstration. Don't overload the learner.

SOME TIPS

☐ Actions speak louder than words in demonstrations.

☐ Don't overload the learner with words while critical actions are being demonstrated.

☐ A demonstration rivets the attention of the learner to what is going on. Always let it speak for itself.

☐ Listening and watching compete for the the attention of the learner.

☐ If you have to talk during demonstrations keep to key attention points, eg 'watch my hands as I do x'.

To illustrate Rule 6 we have some examples (pp 108, 109, 110). These are from instruction which has been recorded onto video-tape. You have the opportunity of seeing a frame-by-frame 'action replay' in slow motion. The clever instructor lets much of the action speak for itself. He lets the learner have the full impact of the demonstration, lets him concentrate wholly on the action, sights and sounds. Notice how words are used sparingly.

Rule 7. A little praise goes a long way

A point often forgotten by instructors is the fundamental importance of praise to the learner. It is easy to think that people learn new skills, jobs and activities for the benefits they will bring — for more money, for personal satisfaction, for the sheer joy of being able to perform the skills satisfactorily.

The essence of these kinds of rewards is that they come only at the end of learning. Only when the learner has learned all of the skill successfully will he be able to experience the thrill (or profit) of doing it himself.

Along the long and often difficult road to learning the learner needs plenty of rewards and gratification. He desperately needs help and encouragement. This can so often only come from you, the instructor.

WHY IS PRAISE SO IMPORTANT?

When they are learning people need to know where they stand, they need to know how they are progressing. The knowledge of their progress spurs them on to greater achievements. In this

106

respect praise is always far more helpful than criticism. We will now examine the specific role of praise in instruction.

A kind word spoken with obvious feeling really does affect people. It makes them feel good. And if they feel good they naturally want to feel that way again; it's as simple as that. And so it goes on. Learners are people, and they love to earn praise from the instructor. Praise is therefore something valuable, to be respected and understood.

LEARNING TO USE PRAISE

It is often said that the real science of instruction lies in understanding how to use praise effectively. This can be easy.

We have firstly to remember that praise can be given in many forms. We can lavish it on the learner in large amounts. We can congratulate him in a forceful and hearty manner. Or we can give more subtle kinds of praise and recognition. No matter how large or how small the amount of praise, one thing is certain: the learner is always intensely aware of it. This is because the instructor is the mirror that the learner uses. Learners measure their progress by the instructor's reactions — especially in the early critical stages of learning.

A good instructor knows this. He will know that the learner depends on him, and that praise can come in many forms. Some kinds of praise work with some people and other kinds with others.

AN EXAMPLE OF THE USE OF PRAISE

I was privileged one day to eavesdrop on a conversation in a workshop going on between a senior instructor and a novice instuctor. The novice instructor had just completed a training course in instruction. In the workshop training was in full swing and we stopped before a class being taught by an experienced instructor how to put a thread onto a steel rod using a die.

The instructor had just carefully demonstrated the technique to the class composed of fifteen mixed adults. The class included a pensioner, an unemployed teenager, a mother of four children and a middle-aged executive.

107

PAIRING INSTRUCTION AND DEMONSTRATION
Demonstrating the golf backswing

'Keep your eye on the ball throughout the backswing. Start your backswing by drawing the club back *inside* the line of flight....

...draw back in as wide an arc as possible. The club is drawn behind you rather than above. Your shoulders and hips are turning. Your right leg is locked, left knee slightly bent....

...full pivot now. Your wrists are fully curled, left arm straight, right arm bent. Your left knee is relaxed.'

PAIRING INSTRUCTION AND DEMONSTRATION
Demonstrating 'boogie-woogie' jazz piano

'Get the left hand
playing the base
line . . .

. . . you've plenty
of time to get
it going . . .

. . . now bring in your
right hand. Play a riff
on the same scale . . .
don't upset your left . . .

. . . keep the left
going, now . . .'

109

PAIRING INSTRUCTION AND DEMONSTRATION

Demonstrating closing the skis into a parallel swing from the snow plough

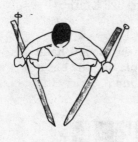

'Transfer your weight onto the right ski, bending your right knee slightly. As you turn on the right ski . . .

. . . the inside ski is naturally turned by your foot. There is little pressure on it . . .

. . . as the skis become parallel keep both knees pressed forward. The inner ski is slightly in advance.'

The learners were just beginning to try the technique of cutting the thread themselves at the workbenches. As a first attempt there were quite naturally some triumphs and some disasters! The instructor was touring the class, carefully guiding the individual learners. At this point I noticed the novice instructor turn to the senior instructor. He whispered:

'It seems to me that the instructor isn't doing anything! He's not even speaking to half of the class. I thought instructors were supposed actively to encourage and praise their learners?'

The senior instructor smiled. 'What this instructor does is really incredible. And he's one of our best instructors. You watch closely. What he does is to give his praise and encouragement in a variety of ways. Listen carefully and above all watch him closely for a few minutes...'

All of us stood and watched. By now the instructor had seen, in turn, well over half the class. 'Look, John – much, much better. But just try to keep the die absolutely horizontal as you rotate it . . .' To another learner he just stopped and watched, absorbed, as she worked on the metal. 'You are getting the knack much better on this exercise, Susan. You are going to be miles ahead of the rest soon.' They both smiled. It was obvious that his comments were part of his strategy of encouraging this particular learner. Susan tackled the next exercise with a glow of pride. The instructor carried on walking round the class. With the next learner he was very different in his style. This time he gave the learner, the teenager, an encouraging pat on the back. As a form of congratulation it went down particularly well for this learner looked as if he had scored his third goal and it was his team mates who were congratulating him. We could all see that the instructor had been particularly inspired in his method of praising this learner.

The feature to strike all three of us onlookers was the immense variety of ways of praising. There was nothing routine and predictable in the instructor's behaviour. Sometimes he would stop and help an ailing learner. He would carefully explain what was wrong then let him start afresh. He would guide by praise and encouragement at every turn. It was close, involved instruction. Yet to another learner, already romping ahead with the exercise, he just gave a breezy word or two. In all it seemed that the instructor was sensitive to just how much praise he needed to give each trainee. He knew also just when to demand better performance by setting challenging tasks.

TIPS FOR USING PRAISE

☐ Praise always makes a learner try to do better. Criticism is usually much less effective in achieving the desired results.

☐ The first attempt by a learner in a task should always be as error-free as possible. This is in order to build up confidence. Have plenty of patience and be liberal with your praise in these early critical stages.

☐ In praise 'variety is the spice of life!' The same routine way of praising people loses its effectiveness with use. Like money, it becomes devalued. Vary your method. Experiment with alternative ways of praising.

☐ Try and find out what kind of praise is most liked by the learner. Adapt your style accordingly (this is discussed more fullly in Chapter 7).

Rule 8. Respect practice!

For all our concern for clarity of objectives and for careful demonstration it is wrong to assume that learning is taking place as the instructor is doing any of these things. Learning only takes place when the learner is actually responding. Instruction is only effective if it requires the learner to respond actively. But even this is not enough. It is not enough simply to tell the learner what is expected, to demonstrate, and then sit back and wait for the correct action to occur. Instruction will be more efficient if the learner can be persuaded and guided to make a response as near as possible to that desired. In order to do this we must follow the principle of 'guided practice' (Merrill 1971). By this we mean a simple scheme to allow the learners to determine for themselves the satisfactoriness of their response as shortly as possible after they make it.

The principle is one of the guiding tenets of much of recent developments in the field of programmed learning, computer-assisted learning and self-instruction. What does it suggest for the instructor? The effective instructor must ask the following questions:

- ☐ When the learner first practises a skill can he readily distinguish his errors after he has finished? Do you as his guide help him to diagnose his errors? Do you talk about these together?
- ☐ Do you try to give immediate feedback as to how well he has performed?
- ☐ Do you show impatience while he tries? Guided practice can only be effective in an unhurried, supportive atmosphere.
- ☐ Have you forgotten the value of humour? Remember that the first practice at a skill is usually an awe-inspiring occasion — be it ski-ing or driving. A joke (never at the expense of the learner) can help reduce tension.

Some good and bad ways of using guided practice periods are compared in the following examples:

GUIDED PRACTICE PERIODS

Poor:

Instructor rapidly describes how to hold a plane. Gives the plane to learners and tells them to plane smooth a plank. Instructor moves away and becomes absorbed in lighting his pipe.

More Effective:

Instructor describes how to hold plane. Lets the learner try. Adjusts learner's finger positions. Instructor takes the plane and demonstrates the forward / backward movement, the weight transfer rhythm. Passes plane to learner. Lets learner imitate a few strokes. Stops him, corrects minor errors...

Instructor demonstrating Padmasana (the Lotus Posture) in Yoga says: 'Watch me.' Sits down quickly. In a rapid series of actions, she folds her legs together. Unfolds them. Then says: 'Try it.'

'Do this slowly, methodically and it comes comfortably. Sit down, relax. Draw your right foot towards your body like this. Do it yourself. Place it sole upwards on your left thigh. Good. Relax. Now take your left foot and draw it up and place it in a similar position upon your right thigh. Do it slowly. Try it. Good. Your left ankle crosses over on top of the right ankle. Hold your spine straight and your chin parallel to the ground.'

113

Conclusion

This chapter has reviewed some of the more important rules the instructor should remember both at the beginning and during instruction:

1. When you first start to instruct, don't put on an act. Don't try and imitate some instructor or teacher you know. You will not succeed. Phoney behaviour on your part will be noticed by the learner. Above all — be yourself!
2. Remember that during instruction it is not the instructor who is important. It is the learner. Talk to him; decide on objectives which are suitable to the learner.
3. Try to get 'inside the skin' of your learner. Try to understand how he feels.
4. Show extra caution when instructing someone emotionally close to you. This is potentially a role-conflict situation and can rapidly get out of hand. Be aware of hurt feelings. Be ready to suggest short instruction sessions spread out over time. This helps keep emotional build-ups under control.
5. Clarity of speech is important in conveying objectives. Carefully match your explanation to demonstration. Let the activity speak for itself where necessary. Don't overburden the learner with information.
6. When giving demonstrations always keep talk to the main points. Do not overload the learner.
7. Learn to respect praise. Learn how to use it with maximum effectiveness for each learner.
8. Try to give as much guidance as possible during initial practice periods. This is when most learning takes place.

References

Anderson, J A (1969) Single-channel and multi-channel messages. *Audio-Visual Communication Review*, 17, 4, 428-434.

Belbin, R M and Belbin, E (1972) *Problems in Adult Retraining*. McGraw-Hill, London.

Department of Employment (1969) *The Training and Use of Operators as Instructors*. HMSO, London.

Hartley, J (1985) *Designing Instructional Text*, Second Edition. Kogan Page, London.

Hsia, H J (1971) The information processing capacity of modality and channel performance. *Audio-Visual Communication Review*, 19, 1, 51-75.

Industrial Training Research Unit (ITRU) (1975) *What's in a Style*. ITRU Publications, Cambridge.

Mager, R F and Clark, C (1963) Explorations in Student-Controlled Instruction. *Psychological Reports*, 13, 71-76.

Mager, R F (1972) On the sequencing of instructional content. In Davies, I K and Hartley, J (eds) *Contributions to an Educational Technology*. Butterworths, London.

Merrill, M D (1971) Paradigms for Psychomoter Instruction. In Merrill, M D (ed) *Instructional Design: Readings*. Prentice-Hall, Englewood Cliffs, New Jersey.

Smith, H C (1966) *Sensitivity to People*. McGraw-Hill, New York.

Smith, P B (1974) The Skills of Interaction. In Dodwell, P C (ed) *New Horizons in Psychology 2*. Penguin, London.

Chapter 7
Adapting your instruction to suit the learner

Overview: Firstly this chapter looks briefly at some of the ways people differ in how they learn. Next it examines some of the more important ways in which instruction can be varied. Finally examples are given on how to adapt instruction to suit the particular needs of the following learners: those who are anxious, the older adult learner, those who are slow to understand instruction.

Introduction

We are all familiar with the fact that people come in various shapes, sizes, ages and colours. We accept that people differ too in their personalities. All these physical and psychological differences add interest and fascination to our daily lives, for it would be a dull world if we were all cast in the same mould.

The area of human differences dealt with in this chapter is not as well known to us as variations in human personality, shapes or sizes. The chapter is about different approaches to learning, different styles of thinking, the different ways people perceive and respond to the world. Let us now see why a knowledge of these is important to the instructor.

Individuals differ

To a certain extent each of us is imprisoned in our own personality and our habits. We all have our own regular ways of behaving. These are so familiar to us that it becomes increasingly difficult to imagine other ways of experiencing and seeing the world — in short, to understand what it is like to be another person.

For example, we are often alarmed or even shocked when one of our friends forms an opinion about a third person which is strongly different from our own view. This can be illustrated further.

How individuals differ

Suppose we were to ask all the readers of this chapter to write down what they have read and understood so far. What might be found if all the responses were gathered together?

We would firstly be struck by the enormous differences in how people organize, remember and understand what they have read. Some people would attempt to recall more or less word-for-word the chapter overview and whole sentences in the chapter itself. Clearly there would be sentences which interested them directly and which stuck in their memory. On the other hand there would be other people who would try and relate to the overall meaning of the chapter so far. They might for instance try to find differences in styles of learning among their friends or children.

In studying the responses we would find two extremes: people concerned with remembering a few details and with getting those details right; at the other extreme would be people more concerned with putting their own interpretation on what they have read. Obviously there would be many people in between these two extremes.

We say that the learner is a unique individual bringing with him to the learning process his own particular lifetime's store of experience, preferences and attitudes. These all result in differing styles of learning and learning needs.

Individual differences in learning have often been ignored

Traditionally the way schools or colleges or training establishments have responded to individual styles of learning has been to ignore or only grudgingly accept them. It was assumed that all people learned in basically the same way. Consequently the same kind of instruction was given to learners regardless of their needs. Cronbach (1967) writing on schools notes:

> Most tactics the school uses are intended to minimize the nuisance
> of individual differences so that it can go on teaching the same
> unaltered course. This is true of remedial instruction which adds
> onto the common programme rather than redesigning it.

Luckily for us the instruction we are concerned with is one-to-one and untroubled by constraints on curricula or school organization. You, the instructor, should be free to give personalized instruction to the learner, the emphasis being on flexibility of instructional style. Let us see how this happens.

Adapting instruction: the experienced instructor

Imagine standing behind a really experienced and successful instructor as he shows a succession of people a particular skill. The skill could be anything: a sports skill, handcraft skill, mechanical or simple tool skill. One striking feature emerges as he proceeds. It is that the instructor behaves noticeably differently with each person. If, for example, the learner starts to stumble over the skill or begins to lose confidence in learning abilities, the instructor will have a number of well tried strategies for raising the learner's confidence. Similarly if a learner is nervous or upset there is an alternative set of tactics to use. Of course the different tactics adopted to suit different learners might appear only slight. Let us examine some.

The strategies which effective instructors use

The instructor might perhaps use a well timed tension-releasing joke with a struggling learner. Perhaps it might be a gentle word or two and a warmer, more accepting tone to a learner given to an attack of nerves. And then again, a crisper, more demanding style might be adopted with an over-confident or. lazy learner.

In the instructional setting these different kinds of behaviour are called instructional strategies and they are a vital and useful tool to any instructor whether novice or experienced (Dallos and Winfield 1975).

We all appreciate that a professional instructor, instructing all day and every day, has ample opportunity to learn how to deal with different types of learners. He can learn by trial and error the best types of instructions to use.

Other people who instruct infrequently, perhaps as part of a hobby or recreational activity, obviously would have limited opportunity to learn how to vary instruction. They want to hit it off correctly with their learner first time. Before we can do this some common ways of varying instruction will be described. But first a word of warning.

The dangers of following fashion

It must be remembered that in noting the following kinds of instruction the reader must not begin to favour any one type over another. In the past education and training has seen many controversies about types of instruction. There were fashions and fads which even today affect our choice of instruction.

The reader is instead reminded that a particular type of instruction might be used only for part of the instructional period. It might well follow a completely different kind of instruction. No conclusion should be drawn about the total educational worth of each type of instruction considered by itself. The instructor should be prepared to be flexible, to select different types, to combine, to try new approaches when old methods are failing.

Varying instruction: high structuring of material

One particular kind of instruction consists in letting the learner know exactly what is required of him at each step. These are often numbered for the convenience of both instructor and learner. For instance you often hear the instructor say 'Firstly you ... next you ... followed by ... finally ...'. When the learner attempts the skill he is closely supervised by an attentive instructor who corrects errors immediately they are made. This is called 'expository instruction' and is the predominant type of instruction in the following examples:

- ☐ Instructing how to operate a pocket calculator/slide rule/camera.
- ☐ Instructing how to position fingers on a typewriter keyboard.
- ☐ Instructing how to build up a long word phonetically.
- ☐ Instructing the general rules of pronunciation.
- ☐ Instructing how to make or undo knots/puzzles/construction kits.

Expository instruction, because of the ordered logical sequence it uses, lends itself well to being written in a programme which learners can work through on their own. This type of instruction can be undertaken in book form, by teaching machine, audio-tape, video tape or practical kit. We can say that if the subject-matter of instruction is technical, mathematical or concerned with logical rules, then there can be found the best and most efficient order in which to present the material (White 1973).

Varying instruction: low structuring of material

In contrast with expository instruction there is instruction which gives only the barest minimum of guidance after the initial setting out of the problem. Here the learner is encouraged to 'have a go' at the skill or problem himself. This is called 'discovery type' instruction:

- ☐ Finding the meaning of an unfamiliar word from the context of a passage with help from an instructor of reading.
- ☐ Finding a 'blown' transistor in an electrical circuit using a voltameter without the aid of circuit diagram.
- ☐ Finding the best balance of fish, temperature, air and vegetation for a successful home aquarium.

Most instruction has both kinds

We realize that most practical instruction involves periods of both discovery and expository instruction. Even in the common examples of giving instructions to someone about a route by car across country; a route by foot up a hill or mountain, or a route by climbing a rock face — all these examples contain the two types for there will be concise, explicit, ordered instructions as well as moments when the learners are left on their own to 'discover' for themselves (Ausubel 1963).

Varying instruction: letting the learner know the results

There is a variety of ways in which an instructor can let the learner know how he is progressing with each attempt at a skill. One way this can vary is in the timing of knowledge of results. The instructor can, for instance, inform the learner of his progress almost continually. Showing someone how to hold hand tools correctly is an example. Alternatively the instructor can let the learner know how he has progressed right at the very end of his attempt or trial. Teaching high board diving, parachute jumping or gymnastics are common examples.

How to instruct when the learner appears anxious or upset

It would be easy to dodge the issue about learner anxiety by offering the simple advice: don't instruct when the learner is anxious. Unfortunately many people, when receiving

121

instruction, do get upset. People obviously differ in how they view the learning process. For instance people who are still receiving education or training usually are not upset by receiving instruction, for they are used to it. On the other hand there are others for whom learning in the past was associated with failure or unhappiness, or whose learning was otherwise unsuccessful or interrupted. Older people long removed from learning environments often show anxiety when placed in these situations (Belbin & Belbin 1972).

How does the instructor recognize learner anxiety?

It is most likely that instructors will have met and talked with their learners before they ever begin to instruct them. This is good, for it gives the instructor a chance to see and meet them in normal relaxed circumstances. If there is a marked difference in the learners' behaviour when instruction actually begins, then anxiety is building up.

Generally speaking people show anxiety by behaviour which is noticeably different from their normal everyday behaviour. A person, normally quite and reserved, when placed in what to him is an anxiety-provoking situation may become excessively talkative. Someone else, perhaps of a more outgoing disposition, may become unnaturally quiet or sullen.

Some clues

Speech, though, is perhaps the best indicator of anxiety in learners, for speech, normally fluent and unbroken, becomes fragmented and unrhythmical. People's bodies can give us clues to anxiety too. Their posture changes, a gradual noticeable stiffening takes place, and there tends to be much reduced use of gesture and body movements. The most important point for the instructor to remember is that the learner's anxiety about a task is not related directly to the difficulty of the task itself. Even the most simple task can present enormous difficulties to the learner. This is a common occurrence. What to the instructor is a recognized simple stage in instruction (say, first handing over a tool for a novice to try) might represent a gigantic anxiety-provoking stage to the learner.

Watch out for anxiety

Anxiety is usually greatest when the learning is accompanied by fear of failure, or loss of face by the learner. The instructor has to be on the lookout for these critical periods. Successful instructors have a number of useful techniques for making the anxious learner more at ease. Here are some for you to use.

TIPS FOR INSTRUCTING THE ANXIOUS LEARNER

☐ Try to use highly structured instruction — avoid discovery approaches where possible.

☐ Let the learner know where he stands as frequently as possible.

☐ Give the learner plenty of emotional support. Give guidance in a warm, accepting manner.

☐ Anxious learners despair at periods of no progress. Let them know that these periods are natural in learning. There is no need to worry, progress will come with steady practice.

☐ Never leave learners to practise for long periods unattended — if they flounder they need help quickly!

☐ Anxious people like to relate to the familiar. Start off your instruction with known topics or with achievements they have themselves made. Alternatively go through little rituals or bantering or jokes that they seem happy with. This helps them forget their anxiety.

☐ Break the learning period up into short, easily managed steps.

☐ Never let a competitive atmosphere enter into your relationship. Never set up comparisons between your student and other learners.

☐ When starting or restarting instruction try and get away from an atmosphere of testing how much they know, have learnt or remembered.

☐ Try and let the pace of instruction be under the control of the learner. Never: 'You ought to be doing X by now!' Rather use gentle nudges to further progress: 'Do you feel ready to tackle X yet?'

Instructing the older adult learner

The story is always the same. The first point all older learners make to their instructor is about their changing ability to learn. Usually they are quick to point out how their ability to learn has decreased as they have grown older.

If we consider the facts, these words must strike us as slightly silly. At present there are more older people successfully learning than at any time in history. They are learning new occupational skills, new trades, new recreational pursuits or following educational courses at a period in life which until a few years ago was considered to be 'too old' for this kind of thing.

What is ageing?

Just what happens to human abilities with advancing age? We often think that the physical motor skills are the earliest to decline, that people slow up in their actions. This is definitely not the case, for the speed of these motor skills of the average 30- to 50-year-old is very nearly as high as that of the average adolescent. Even between 50 and 69 there is only a negligible difference. In fact certain specific practical abilities and language-based skills appear hardly to decline at all with age.

Special care needed

All that happens with increasing age is that the older person just needs a little more time to grasp the meaning of a new unfamiliar situation — especially if it is at all complex. An unfamiliar lay-out of instruments and controls in a new car, a new format and print lay-out for an application form, the controls on a redesigned power tool; all these are examples of learning situations needing care. Older people can, and do, of course respond with the appropriate physical output demanded by the situation (Chapter 3) — they only require just a little longer to decide what to do. In short the slowing up appears to be central, in the brain, rather than any loss of sensitivity or muscle power.

Danger spots in learning are when the information or happenings are occurring too fast. This applies whether it is visual information, speech or symbols. Any situation, in fact, where the older person must make a conscious decision about what to do.

Older people learn differently

Studies of older people learning new skills — physical or intellectual — show that they can, and do, compensate for this decline in central information processing powers.

For instance they will concentrate harder, exclude everything else from their attention; they will take more time to survey thoroughly the situation before they react; they will perform more checks on what they have just done. Altogether they learn and progress with a little more hesitation and caution.

How old is older?

For the purposes of instruction it can be said that as a rough guide if the learner is over 40 years old it is worthwhile considering adapting instruction to allow for the differences in mental ability. A careful instructor paying heed to a few simple tips can make an older learner romp through even the most complex learning task. It is a feat achieved daily in many countries where people of 60 to 65 are happily learning totally new trades. Adult illiterates over 50 are increasingly being successfully instructed in reading skills.

Pace is important

The guiding rule for the instructor lies in the pace of presentation of the learning material, not a slowing down in the rate of speech by instructing deliberately slowly. That would be insulting to the learner. Rather, it is better to allow an increase in the time allowed to grasp or understand. The instructor must above all try and get into the mental framework of the older learner, try and learn the pace that suits his learner best. Here are some ways you can modify your instruction:

TIPS FOR INSTRUCTING THE OLDER LEARNER

☐ Try and avoid instruction which relies on the conscious memorization of long wordy rules. For example in spelling using the rules of combinations of letters. Try instead to let examples of correct spelling drive home the rule.

☐ Give the learner a chance to show mastery of one part of the learning task before moving on to the next.

☐ Try and correct early errors — they have a habit of persisting with older learners.

☐ Choose learning tasks that give instant success. For example with an adult illiterate choose the 'look-say' method using everyday written familiar material.

TIPS FOR INSTRUCTING THE OLDER LEARNER *(continued)*

☐ Try and instruct in meaningful 'whole' parts of a task rather than in little portions which may seem unconnected.

☐ Always be ready to vary the method of instruction. Always do this instead of needless repetitions which can tire the adult learner.

☐ It sometimes helps to try the discovery methods of instruction — but be sure you give them carefully graded discovery tasks.

☐ Don't alter the logic of presentation of a task. As an example: demonstrating how to tie a knot directly in front of the learner then asking them to substitute right for left, left for right when they attempt it.

☐ Always allow the learner to dictate the pace of learning.

☐ Beware of interrupted learning-sessions, remember that they cause forgetfulness in older learners.

☐ Older learners seem to prefer longer periods of instruction rather than short periods. It is better to have sessions of an hour or more, than short five- or ten-minute periods.

☐ Try and devise simple aids which allow learners to spot their own mistakes before they become bad habits. For example let an adult poor speller compare his response with a correctly spelt word.

Instructing the slow learner

When an instructor has someone in his charge who is experiencing learning difficulties he must be more than ever aware of learner needs. One false step can be disastrous here, because it does not take much to crush the will to learn. Difficulties of concentration, slow rates of learning with little sense of achievement all add up to a more than ready willingness on the part of the slow learner to throw up the sponge.

Common errors among instructors

One common error often made by instructors who have had little or no training in instructing the slow learner, is as follows. They will explain once, twice, three times. Each time their explanations will become more lengthy and elaborate. During the course of these explanations the instructor often unknowingly varies the vocabulary used — with the result that no sooner has the learner learnt the word to label correctly some tool, action or object, than the instructor uses a synonym.

The blank look of bafflement on the face of the learner is living proof of the instructor's failure to be prepared to vary instructional method to suit the demands of the learner.

TIPS FOR INSTRUCTING THE SLOW LEARNER

☐ Always use small learning steps.

☐ Give plenty of praise and encouragement for success no matter how small the success seems to you.

☐ Slow learners are often easily distracted. Create a calm working atmosphere that they can come to respect. For example if instructing an adult illiterate clear away things from a table, place a lamp on it and arrange books and learning material in an orderly fashion. This activity prepares the learner for learning; the learning area you have created helps to focus his attention.

☐ Keep your explanations brief. Slow learners have difficulty with dense, wordy instruction.

☐ Use the same words for labelling throughout your instruction.

☐ Short learning sessions avoid possible boredom and discouragement.

☐ Try to have a set routine of instruction which the learner can come to look forward to.

☐ Give plenty of opportunity for practice to ensure learning has taken place.

Conclusion

When you instruct in one-to-one situations you need to be ready beforehand. You need to be prepared to offer the individual learner exactly what he needs from the learning experience. Not, that is, what you as an instructor believe they need; rather to offer that specific kind of instruction which is best suited to their own unique learning needs.

Other learners with special needs

Although this chapter has talked about instructing three special types of learner — slow learners, anxious or under-confident learners and older learners — clearly learners come with a far wider variety of special needs. They come over-confident; they come tired or dispirited; they come hurried or upset by outside events; they come young and impatient, to name but a few. Although we are not as yet able to generalize and offer guidance on how to instruct these and many other types of learners, we are however certain of one thing.

Flexibility and adaptability matter most

Instructors need every time to be ready to adapt and to cope. They need to be ready to drop one approach if it fails to bring success, and to try another. Instructors need a genuine willingness to pick and choose between the different types of instructional methods mentioned in this chapter.

This readiness to innovate, this boldness to abandon and try afresh with a new approach — this is the essence of successful adaptive instruction.

References

Ausubel, D P (1963) *The Psychology of Meaningful Verbal Learning*. Grune and Stratton, London.

Belbin, E and Belbin, R M (1972) *Problems in Adult Retraining*. Heinemann, London.

Cronbach, L J (1967) How can instruction be adapted to individual differences? In Gagné, R M (ed) *Learning and Individual Differences*. Merrill, Columbus.

Dallos, R and Winfield, I (1975) Instructional Strategies in Industrial Training and Rehabilitation. *Journal of Occupational Psychology*, 48, 4, 241-252.

White, R J (1973) Research into learning hierarchies. *Review of Educational Research*, Summer, 43, 3, 361-376.

Further reading

Ansley, J and Ennis M (1980) *REACH. Residential Electrical Wiring Units*. Georgia University, Atlanta, US. Division of Vocational Education.

Bishop, F (1979) *Industrial Mechanics Occupational Cluster Guide*. Oregon State Department of Education, Salem, US.

Brown, S (1977) Taking Senior Citizens off the Shelf. *Worklife* 2, 3, 14-19.

Buffer, J J (1979) Industrial Arts and Consumer Education. *Man, Society, Technology*, 39, 3, 28-29.

Butler, R H *et al* (1981) *Mechanical Technology. Post Secondary Curriculum Guide*. Georgia University, Atlanta, US. Division of Vocational Education.

English, C *et al* (1980) *REACH. Major Appliance*. Georgia University, Atlanta, US. Division of Vocational Education.

Grouse, J (1979) Mom's the Sewing Teacher. *Momentum* 10, 2, 50.

Hall, E J and Turner, R C (1975) *An Analysis of the Industrial mechanics Occupation*. Ohio State Department of Education. Columbus University, US.

Henderson W C *et al* (1973) *General Mechanical Trades. A Curriculum Guide. Revised Edition*. Oklahoma State Department of Vocational and Technical Education, Stillwater Curriculum and Instructional Materials Centre.

Hoerner, T A (1979) Skills, Skills, or Skills? *Agricultural Educational Magazine* 51, 11, 246-47.

ITRU (1976) *Choose an Effective Style: a self-instructional approach to the teaching of skills*. ITRU Research paper TR9.

Peace Corps (1981) *Remote Areas Development Manual. Appropriate Technologies for Development*. Peace Corps, Information Collection and Exchange Division. Washington DC, US.

Scanlon, J A (1983) *Development of a Set of Curriculum Materials for the Implementation of an Instructional Strategy for Teaching Basic Mechanical Skills in Exploratory Vocational Agriculture Classes. Final Report*. Arkansas University Project of Vocational Education.

Smith, A De W (1979) *Generic Skills. Trade Families*. Canadian Commission of Employment and Immigration. Ottawa, Ontario, Canada.

Smith, G *et al* (1980) *REACH. Electricity Units, Post-Secondary*. Georgia University, Atlanta, US. Division of Vocational Education.

Stanfield, C *et al* (1980) *REACH. Heating Units*. Georgia University, Atlanta, US. Division of Vocational Education.

United Nations Educational, Scientific and Cultural Organisation (1980) *Vocational and Technical Education*. UNESCO Regional Office for Education in Asia and Oceania, Bangkok, Thailand.

White, C B (1983) Early Adolescence: Practical Technology. *Science and Children*. 21, 2, 38-41.